Presented to:

A COMPLETE GUIDE TO BIBLICAL

Fasting

Also by Ted Shuttlesworth Jr.

*Further Faster: How to Accelerate Your Purpose
Through the Force of Impartation*

*Unhang Your Harp: How Praise Opens the Door to
Every Blessing God Has Provided for You*

Blood on the Door: The Protective Power of Covenant

Blood on the Door: Workbook

*Praise. Laugh. Repeat.: Living in the Power
of Overwhelming Joy*

*Praise. Laugh. Repeat. Devotional:
A 40-Day Journey to Overwhelming Joy*

(Also available on Apple Books and Amazon Kindle)

A COMPLETE GUIDE TO BIBLICAL

MASTER THE HABIT

that provokes

GOD'S FAVOR

TED SHUTTLESWORTH JR.

MIRACLE WORD
PUBLISHING

Published in Virginia Beach, Virginia by Miracle Word Publishing.

Miracle Word titles may be purchased in bulk for educational, business, fund-raising, or sales promotional use. For information, please e-mail info@miracleword.com

Scripture quotations marked (NLT) are taken from the Holy Bible, New Living Translation, copyright ©1996, 2004, 2015 by Tyndale House Foundation. Used by permission of Tyndale House Publishers, Carol Stream, Illinois 60188. All rights reserved.

Scripture quotations marked NKJV are from the NEW KING JAMES VERSION. © 1982 by Thomas Nelson, Inc. Used by permission. All rights reserved.

Scripture quotations taken from the New American Standard Bible®, Copyright © 1960, 1962, 1963, 1968, 1971, 1972, 1973, 1975, 1977, 1995 by The Lockman Foundation Used by permission." (www.Lockman.org)

Scripture quotations are from the ESV® Bible (The Holy Bible, English Standard Version®), copyright © 2001 by Crossway, a publishing ministry of Good News Publishers. Used by permission. All rights reserved.

Scripture quoted by permission. Quotations designated (NET) are from the NET Bible® copyright ©1996, 2019 by Biblical Studies Press, L.L.C. http://netbible.com All rights reserved.

All uppercase and italicized text in verses of scripture are added by the author for the purpose of emphasis.

ISBN 978-1-7349962-2-7

Printed in the United States of America

For the Partners of this ministry — The Victory Tribe. Never-ending increase is yours.

CONTENTS

FOREWORD

Ted Shuttlesworth Jr. comes from a family that not only teaches prayer and fasting, but they practice the discipline of fasting. Ted has seen the discipline required of fasting and has experienced the rewards and victory that make the pain and difficulties of not eating worth it all.

A Complete Guide to Biblical Fasting has an underlying theme that the discipline of fasting is the hidden key that creates history makers. There was a reason Jesus fasted for 40 days. If he could have received the same results in his ministry only by praying and using his faith, he would have never fasted.

However, there are some miracles and breakthroughs that only abstaining from food bring. The New Testament would have been quite a bit shorter if Jesus had not fasted. He would not have walked on water, raised Lazarus from the dead, cast out the demons into the herd of pigs, nor multiplied the loaves and fishes.

Dr. Yonggi Cho was dying of tuberculosis at 17 years of age. A schoolmate gave him a Bible. When he read about the miracles, he asked Jesus to heal him. His father threw him out of his Buddhist home. He started preaching in a tent that eventually grew to the world's largest church with over a million members.

His mother-in-law, Madam Che, once said to my father and me, "The secret of our church growing to over a million members is to "pray, pray, pray and fast, fast, fast."

In this book, Ted Shuttlesworth Jr. explains how fasting releases not only natural blessings, but supernatural miracles. It extends your life, causes your hair to grow, is one of the most powerful healing agents to cancer, brings prosperity, increases your prayer power, breaks demonic strongholds, heals family issues, breaks addictions, brings deliverance from homosexuality, releases wisdom and solutions to impossible situations, stirs up the gifts of the Holy Spirit, discharges angels to work on your behalf, and much more.

When I first began my journey of fasting, I was 22 years old. I didn't know anybody who fasted. I broke every rule and failed in my fasting efforts more than any other person. The church I pastored ran 40 people. In 30 days, after I began fasting one day a week, the church "grew" to 20 people. For me to grow, I had to have a backdoor revival first.

Since then, fasting has opened doors in my life. I've preached in 47 countries, pastor a church of over 9,000 members, preached at the largest church in the world, the largest Presbyterian Church in the world, the largest Methodist Church in the world, and own over seven TV stations and seven radio stations. None of this would ever have been accomplished without the breakthrough key of fasting. Are the discomfort and struggles of a fast worth it? Absolutely.

I encourage you to not only read this book but study and practice it. Begin a life of fasting. When you do, buckle your seatbelt because God is getting ready to take you to places where few people have ever gone. This may be the most important book you will read this year outside of the Bible.

—Dr. Bob Rodgers
Pastor, Evangel World Prayer Center; Author, *101 Reasons to Fast* and *The 21-Day Fast*

There will never be a convenient time to fast. You have to dedicate your time to the Lord.

Chapter One

10 REASONS TO FAST AND PRAY

It was the middle of winter in Virginia Beach, Virginia. I was in my early twenties and on staff as an associate in my uncle, Pastor Terry Shuttlesworth's church.

As a leader, he always emphasized fasting and prayer and still does today. We wouldn't just fast once a year in January; we would spend three days fasting with special prayer services each month.

If you think about it, giving God three days of fasting and prayer every month is thirty-six days of fasting. That's a tithe of your year given to the Lord in consecration. This is a simple pattern that could be added to any believer's life.

There was only one problem—I hated fasting. I couldn't stand it. Though I grew up in a Christian environment, I (like many others) didn't understand the benefits and power of fasting and prayer. I looked for any reason I could find to get out of fasting.

"After today, I felt a release in my spirit," I would often say, leveraging hyper-spiritual jargon with which no one could argue. Then, I'd eat again.

Three days of fasting can quickly turn into one day, and one-day can slip into one-meal. Before you know it, you're never fasting. It's amazing how many reasons your flesh can find to cancel or break a fast.

It's important to remember that there will never be a convenient time to fast. Let me reiterate that.

There will never be a convenient time to fast.

There will always be a work dinner, a birthday party, a holiday, or some event that can become an excuse to cancel your fast. Ignore them. If people don't understand, that's their problem. You have to obey the Lord.

I can remember sitting in the office with my stomach growling. I couldn't focus because I just kept thinking about food. I quickly made an excuse about having to run an errand and walked to my car.

I drove across town to an area where I didn't think anybody would recognize me, especially people from the church who were also fasting. I zoomed into a 7-11 parking lot and ran inside where I was greeted by the smell of monterey jack chicken taquitos. I grabbed the special, three for five dollars, and quickly checked out.

I had already eaten half of the first taquito before they swiped my credit card. By the time I was in the car, I was polishing off the last of the bag.

That's when the guilt and repentance set in. I vowed to go back on the fast and be faithful this time. I was going to press in like never before. Days later, with Big Mac special sauce on my lips and grease-stained, salty, french fry fingers, I felt bad again.

THE WHY DRIVES THE WHAT

The problem that kept me inconsistent and frequently failing is that I didn't understand *why* we fast and pray. I viewed fasting only as a religious duty and was oblivious to the many benefits that accompanied it. As long as the purposes were obscured from me, I would miss out on the many blessings.

In his best-selling book, *Start With Why*, author Simon Sinek reveals the powerful implications of understanding *why* something is done or a product is made.

The why is always more engaging and productive than the what or the how. In what he calls the "Golden Circle," a target made up of three rings, he outlines the three areas where corporations or individuals focus.

The outer ring, which is the biggest circle, is the *what*.

Everyone knows what they do. That doesn't set you apart, nor does it inspire you to go further. Additionally, it would never inspire others to follow you.

The middle ring is the *how*. This narrows the focus a bit. Though everyone knows what they do, some don't understand how they do it in such a way that sets them apart from their competition.

Finally, the inner circle—the bullseye—is the *why*. Very few people understand this. However, when you understand it and make it the focal point of all you do, it brings overwhelming drive and success.

Sinek uses Apple Computers as an example of starting with why. Instead of simply saying, "We make great computers. They're beautifully designed and easy to use. Wanna buy one?" They press deeper into the why of their corporation in a way that builds a following. It becomes a brand with a purpose.

Instead, Apple says, "We believe in challenging the status quo and thinking differently. We do that by making our products beautiful and simple-to-use. We just happen to make great computers. Wanna buy one?" The why is far more inspiring than the what or how.[1]

The same is true for fasting. When I simply engaged in the what (fasting) and knowing the how (by not eating), I failed to successfully complete my goals.

However, when I truly learned the why of fasting, it

sparked a hunger within me to do it faithfully and lead others — like you as you read this book — to do it with me.

Maybe this will be the most poignant section of the book for you because you've never fully understood the many benefits fasting brings. Perhaps like me, you've missed the why. The following will open your eyes.

This chapter will outline the Old and New Testament purposes of fasting as well as the supernatural benefits that follow as you dedicate yourself to the Lord. Although fasting also produces natural health benefits for your body, we will cover those separately.

Before we begin, it's important to remember that some of the reasons for fasting in the Old Testament aren't the same in the New. The blood of Christ made permanent changes that cause us to act differently than Old Testament saints did. I'll explain these differences as we go along.

PURPOSE 1: PURE OBEDIENCE

When we ask ourselves the question, "Why should I fast?" The most straightforward answer is, "Because Jesus said so." If that were the only reason we fasted, it would be more than enough. Of course, there are more elements that make up the purpose of fasting along with many benefits. However, we must begin here.

The commands of Scripture must direct everything we do. These commands are the expectations of God for his children. As we cover in the chapter, *Is Fasting Necessary for New Testament Believers*, Jesus outlines his expectations for his followers in the future. He said that after he was taken from them, they would fast.

> *"The days will come when the bridegroom is taken away from them, and then they will fast in those days."*
> **Luke 5:35 ESV**

This was Jesus' answer to the question about why his disciples weren't fasting in a time when the Pharisees and John's disciples were.

There's no way to read Christ's answer and conclude that believers aren't required to fast or shouldn't think seriously about it. To say you don't need to fast is to say you're not truly a disciple of Christ since a life of fasting is one of the elements that defines discipleship.

While you're not required to follow any specific fasting schedule, fasting isn't something that should be done only once a year or flippantly as an afterthought.

As you discover the purposes of fasting in this chapter, it will help you determine when and how you should dedicate yourself to fasting and prayer.

PURPOSE 2: EMULATE THE MASTER

Throughout the Scripture, we can see that God used men to lead the Body of Christ by example. That's what true discipleship is — training others to emulate the disciplines of their master.

Many people know the name Bruce Lee, world-famous movie star, and Kung Fu master, but very few would recognize the name Ip Kai-man.

Master Ip was a famous Chinese martial artist who specialized in the Wing Chun style of Kung Fu. When Ip was 16, he moved to Hong Kong to attend St. Stephen's, a secondary school for foreigners or wealthy families.

About six months after he moved, a classmate told Ip that a Kung Fu master — a friend of his father — was living at his house. At the time, Ip was undefeated (and probably a bit arrogant.)

One Sunday afternoon, he went to his classmate's house, exchanged brief pleasantries with the Kung Fu master, and then promptly challenged him to a duel.

His opponent, Leung Bik, easily overwhelmed and defeated Ip. Not able to believe how quickly he was defeated, he challenged Leung to a rematch, but he was beaten just as deftly as before.

Discouraged, he left the house. Afterward, Ip was so depressed he wouldn't even admit that he knew Kung

Fu. Later, it was revealed that Leung Bik, who defeated him, was the son of the man who had trained Ip's master, Chan Wah-shun.

With that knowledge, a recharged Ip continued in that discipline and became a master himself. He trained many notable students, including the Green Hornet's famous sidekick Kato — played by Bruce Lee.[2]

Notice it's the emulation of the master's disciplines that brings success. This isn't a martial arts concept; it's a biblical one.

The Apostle Paul, who the Lord used to shape the first-century church, used this principle extensively. Twice, he encouraged the Corinthian believers to imitate his life and disciplines (1 Corinthians 4:16; 11:1).

It was such an important concept that even when Paul wasn't with the church members, he would sometimes send his own disciples to continue to train them.

> *That is why I sent you Timothy, my beloved and faithful child in the Lord, to remind you of my ways in Christ, as I teach them everywhere in every church.*
> *1 Corinthians 4:17 ESV*

I find it interesting and informative that the first thing the Holy Spirit led Jesus to do after he was filled with the Spirit was to fast and pray. That was no accident. It's a pattern to be viewed by those of us who follow him.

As I cover in the chapters about New Testament believers and the Apostle Paul, Jesus set an example and expectation of fasting that has been followed by the church since he left the earth.

If we want to do the works Jesus did and greater, we must emulate his disciplines, as well. (See John 14:12.)

PURPOSE 3: TO HUMBLE YOURSELF

If you've been a Christian for any period of time, you've heard the phrase, "Pride goes before a fall." It's become a commonly uttered but shortened version of Proverbs 16:18. Pride goes before destruction, and a haughty spirit before a fall.

The Bible is full of stories of individuals and nations being brought low because of unbridled pride. As I cover in a separate chapter, pride makes you God's opponent. He opposes the proud (James 4:6). Humility, on the other hand, attracts his presence and blessings. Notice how the Lord promised to deal with his people during the reign of Solomon:

> *If my people who are called by my name*
> *humble themselves, and pray and seek*

9

my face and turn from their wicked
ways, then I will hear from heaven and
will forgive their sin and heal their land.
2 Chronicles 7:14 ESV

God requires humility from those who seek his favor. Notice it's the first thing he requires in this verse. Throughout the Old Testament, fasting was a form of humbling yourself.

In times when David's sin was being judged, he would put on sackcloth and humble himself with fasting (Psalm 35:13). His zeal for God caused this to happen often (Psalm 69:10).

One of the most dangerous mistakes any Christian can make is the trap of self-dependence. When we stop recognizing we depend on the Lord for everything, we can quickly become prideful. That mistake carries a curse.

Thus says the LORD: "Cursed is the man
who trusts in man and makes flesh his
strength, whose heart turns away from
the LORD.
Jeremiah 17:5 ESV

Fasting weakens our flesh and puts our total focus back on the Lord. Fasting is a way of saying with our stomach and our whole body how much we need, want, and trust Jesus.

Ezra, the Old Testament scribe and priest, was tasked with leading a group of exiled Jews from Persia back to the newly-rebuilt Jerusalem.

He made up his mind, however, that they wouldn't depend on themselves for protection and a successful journey. He led God's people in humbling themselves.

> *Then I proclaimed a fast there, at the river Ahava, that we might humble our-selves before our God, to seek from him a safe journey for ourselves, our children, and all our goods.*
>
> *Ezra 8:21 ESV*

Your flesh nature will try to strengthen itself. It will demand the things that it wants. The stronger it be-comes, and the more you allow it to have what it wants, the more you will fulfill the lusts of the flesh. (See Galatians 5:16-17.) Nothing weakens your flesh more quick-ly than depriving it of calories.

The weakening—or humbling—of the flesh allows your spirit to be heard and take control. This is why cre-ating some sort of a fasting schedule (as the first-century church did) rather than fasting only once a year is more effective and makes more sense.

People will try to define you as super-spiritual if you fast often. Some may even mock you, asking, "Is that much fasting necessary?"

Since we recognize fasting as a Christian discipline modeled and commanded by Christ, we can conclude it's as necessary as any other.

Can you imagine mocking a Christian for praying or reading the Bible every day? Would you try to "talk some sense" into a Christian who attended church faithfully every week? Would you tell a Christian to calm down because they were winning souls every day? No.

That's how foolish it is to view a life of consistent fasting as excessive. We must subdue our flesh daily. Humbling yourself is a discipline that must be done continually. Fasting is the quickest route to humble yourself before the Lord.

PURPOSE 4: TO EXPRESS GRIEF

In the Old Testament, fasting was a way to show extreme grief. Even now, when people deal with situations that provoke grief or heartbreak, they lose their appetite, and some may not eat for days.

In 2 Samuel, we have an example of this kind of fasting as David and his men learn of Saul and Jonathan's death.

And they mourned and wept and fasted
until evening for Saul and for Jonathan
his son and for the people of the LORD
and for the house of Israel, because they
had fallen by the sword.

                    2 Samuel 1:12 ESV

After the battle in question had finished and the valiant men of Jabesh-gilead found Saul and his sons, they carried their bodies to Jabesh, burned them, buried their bones under a tree, and fasted for seven days. (See 1 Samuel 31:13.)

Except for feeling grief for the state of the wicked world or the desire for your generation to be changed, we don't see grief expressed the same way among New Testament believers.

When loved ones die, as in the case of David discovering Jonathan's death, we don't grieve as unbelievers would; we rejoice knowing that our loved ones are in Heaven with the Lord. If our loved ones weren't saved, there is no point in fasting or praying because we're unable to change the situation through prayer.

I'm sure the Lord would be pleased with this sobering position of grief for sin in the New Testament church. However, I believe we would be better served fasting and praying to consecrate our lives to God and to be em-

powered to preach the gospel of Christ to a lost and dying world. That's something David and Old Testament
saints could not do.

PURPOSE 5: TO SUPPLEMENT REPENTANCE

In the New Testament, Saul (who later became Paul)
fasted for three days after his encounter with the Lord
on the road to Damascus.

As I cover in the chapter about the Apostle Paul, some
argue that Saul spent his three days of fasting in deep
mourning as he was confronted with the realization that
although he thought he was doing the Lord's work by
persecuting the newly-formed Christian church, he was
fighting against God himself.

Imagine the deep grief you'd feel if you thought
you'd spent your entire life faithfully serving God, and
then discovering what you were doing was extremely
displeasing to him. You would be in a state of shock, too.

Additionally, though Saul had to repent and be
saved, fasting is not the method for repentance. Although godly sorrow produces repentance (2 Corinthians 7:10), fasting is not the act of repentance; it's the act
of expressing sorrow for your actions. However, as Paul
taught the Corinthians, what good is sorrow if it doesn't
produce a change in your life?

No Christian should be living a life of constant sin. Paul instructed the Romans to live free from sin since it no longer had dominion over them (Romans 6:1-14).

If you're living a life that's so displeasing to God that you must fast to express grief for your ongoing wickedness, there are severe problems, and you need to rededicate your life to the Lord in salvation.

In Saul's example, I should reiterate that *he was not a believer* at the time of his encounter with God. Only after fasting and his meeting with Ananias was he baptized and filled with the Spirit.

I stress this because fasting isn't a prescription for repentance in the life of a believer. John wrote:

> *If we confess our sins, he is faithful and*
> *just to forgive us our sins . . .*
> *1 John 1:9 ESV*

However, as humility is a critical element in the life of any believer, a life of continued fasting will keep your flesh in subjection and repentance far less frequent.

PURPOSE 6: FOR DISCIPLINE

As I cover in the chapter on the natural benefits of fasting, many people physically suffer because they have made unwise decisions with their body.

A large number of health problems people are facing could be eliminated by taking control of their desire for food. Cancer, heart disease, strokes, diabetes, hypertension, and high blood pressure could be avoided by wise choices and self-control. Paul spoke of the belly as a god that must be defeated.

> *Their end is destruction, their god is their*
> *belly, and they glory in their shame, with*
> *minds set on earthly things.*
> *Philippians 3:19 ESV*

Your flesh not only wants to overeat, but it also wants to eat anything it likes. Children (and many adults) left to their own devices won't choose to steam broccoli and cauliflower as a go-to snack or meal. They reach for candy, chips, pizza, and other forms of junk food. The command to discipline your body is not some form of "self-help" message; it's a scriptural principle. Let me show you something that will change the way you think about your body.

> *Or do you not know that your body is*
> *a temple of the Holy Spirit within you,*
> *whom you have from God? You are not*

> *your own, for you were bought with a*
> *price. So glorify God in your body.*
> *1 Corinthians 6:19-20 ESV*

How would you prepare a room in your house if you knew the Holy Spirit was coming to stay with you? Would you put him in the damp, cold basement on an old, blow-up mattress? No. I'm sure you'd give him the best room in the house and furnish it with as many up-grades as you could, creating the best experience possible for the Holy Spirit.

If that's true, why do we treat our bodies—his dwelling place—so flippantly? Part of what fasting does is allow us to control our flesh and curb unhealthy eating.

In his infinite wisdom, God knew the positive effects fasting would have on our bodies. Not only do we get to experience the spiritual benefits, but obeying the command of Christ to fast strengthens our bodies, as well.

PURPOSE 7: TO WORSHIP GOD

While not commonly mentioned, one of the purposes of fasting is to express love and worship to the Lord. We often view fasting as a tool to expedite or strengthen prayer but don't realize God views it as worship.

While they were worshiping the Lord and fasting, the Holy Spirit said, "Set apart for me Barnabas and Saul for the work to which I have called them."
Acts 13:2 ESV

Hunger expresses desire. That's why it means so much when we direct our hunger toward God. As Jesus said in Matthew, a blessing comes upon those who hunger (Matthew 5:6).

As one author aptly wrote, "What we hunger for most, we worship."[3] We have the opportunity to be hungrier for God than we are for food.

As the lack of strength from no calories is the loudest objection your body can make, it only makes sense that fasting with prayer is one of the strongest forms of worship that there is. Look at Anna, a prophetess in the New Testament.

And there was a prophetess, Anna . . . She did not depart from the temple, worshiping with fasting and prayer night and day.
Luke 2:36-37 ESV

Imagine the depths of worship that could be reached by continually fasting and praying throughout your life as a believer. I believe that many issues that others are forced to pray about would simply vanish in the lives of those who stayed in deep communion with the Lord.

PURPOSE 8: TO EXPRESS CONCERN FOR THE WORK OF THE LORD

A.A. Allen, the mighty tent evangelist, was very dissatisfied with the results of his ministry. He didn't see the miracles, signs, or wonders that he desired so much. The number of salvations were not what he expected. He was disheartened and needed a breakthrough.

He made up his mind that he would fast and pray until God began to move in his ministry. He locked himself in his prayer closet and began to seek the Lord. Not long after, Jesus appeared to him and began to speak to him concerning his life and ministry.

Jesus gave him a checklist, which he wrote down. These were things he needed to do for the Lord to use him in the miracle ministry. He writes:

"As the time passed, I have marked the requirements from my list, one by one. The list grew smaller and smaller as I shouted the victory over Satan."[4]

I include the full excerpt of his story in the next chapter, but Allen's concern for the work of the Lord propelled him into fasting and prayer, and it should do the same for us. Nehemiah also felt the urgency of completing the Lord's work.

> *And they said to me, ". . . The wall of Je-rusalem is broken down . . . " As soon as I heard these words I sat down and wept and mourned for days, and I continued fasting and praying before the God of heaven.*
> *Nehemiah 1:3-4 ESV*

When God has placed a call upon your life, you will feel the burden of that call. Many times fasting and prayer are the initial response to the burden you feel for the call of God you've been given and the work you've been assigned.

PURPOSE 9: TO PREPARE FOR MINISTRY

Without question, the ministry is taken too lightly in this generation. Some take a very fleshly approach to ministry, treating it much like a business.

Although ministry requires business sense and knowledge, it is a spiritual venture. It's a dangerous thing to enter into ministry if you're not called to do it.

In the Bible, fasting and prayer were necessary prerequisites for full-time ministry.

Acts 13 illustrates this principle, but it's an interesting example that shows the gravity of stepping into ministry.

> *While they were worshiping the Lord and fasting, the Holy Spirit said, "Set apart for me Barnabas and Saul for the work to which I have called them." Then after fasting and praying they laid their hands on them and sent them off.*
> *Acts 13:2-3 ESV*

I want you to notice that during their fasting and worship, the Holy Spirit spoke to them about who to separate into the ministry. However, they didn't instantly separate them.

Only after a second period of fasting did they lay hands on Saul and Barnabas and send them out to minister.

I believe that a combination of things we've covered in this chapter factor into the ministry preparation equation. Humility and consecration are necessary for successful ministry, as are concern for God's work and a desire to emulate your master.

I don't say this lightly, but with the many purposes and benefits tied to fasting in Scripture, I question the dedication, passion, and hunger of any full-time minister who does not make biblical fasting a regular part of their spiritual life.

Although you may consider that too harsh of a statement, how would you view a doctor who refused to study at medical school and knew nothing of healthcare procedures? What about a lawyer who wouldn't stay current with changes in state or federal laws?

They are ill-prepared for any encounters in their respective fields of expertise. The same is true with ministers who refuse to dedicate themselves to fasting as Jesus commanded in the New Testament.

PURPOSE 10: TO ESTABLISH CHURCHES AND MINISTRIES

Not only was fasting used to separate ministers unto the Lord, but it was also something that was done before churches or ministries were established in the New Testament. It's important to remember that Christ is the head of the church. Believers shouldn't try to assume that role.

Establishing a church or ministry is Christ's business. It's my opinion many churches fail because they were the vision of a man, not the mandate of God. Look what Jesus said about building the church:

And I tell you, you are Peter, and on this
rock I will build my church, and the gates
of hell shall not prevail against it.
Matthew 16:18 ESV

Christ will build *his* church. If someone who God never called into the ministry decides to force their way in and launch their own church or ministry, God isn't required to provide for that vision. God only pays for what he orders. Pride can make people do dangerous things that will cost them dearly.

On the other hand, if God has called you, no other choice can compare to the greatness of being a servant of God. As the famous Baptist pastor Charles Spurgeon, known as the "Prince of Preachers," said, "If God has called you to be his servant, why stoop to be a king?"

After Saul and Barnabas were sent out to minister, they began appointing elders in the churches, but not without fasting and prayer.

And when they had appointed elders for
them in every church, with prayer and
fasting they committed them to the Lord
in whom they had believed.
Acts 14:23 ESV

23

When my uncle, Pastor Terry Shuttlesworth, felt to plant a church in Virginia, he spent much time in fasting and prayer. As I previously mentioned, the church would fast corporately for three days every month. In addition, at the beginning of the year, we would seek the Lord in twenty-one days of fasting and prayer.

I saw my uncle engage in many times of fasting and prayer, including a forty-day fast. We watched as the Lord caused the church to multiply. Though the church was launched from nothing, it quickly grew to over five hundred people in a short time.

Before you make any major decision in your life, you should fast and pray.

We can find many reasons to fast throughout the Bible, but because churches rarely teach on fasting, many are unaware of all the Bible has to say about it.

Now that you understand the biblical reasons *why* we fast, we'll discuss the supernatural benefits of fasting and prayer.

Chapter Two

THE SUPERNATURAL POWER OF SELF-DENIAL

In the earlier part of my ministry, I began to ask the Lord to manifest his power in a greater measure in our meetings. I would pray for great miracles, signs, and wonders to take place in each revival.

One day, as I was praying, the Lord said to me, "You've gone as far as you can go at your current level of prayer." I felt like he slapped me in the face.

Your flesh wants to shout, "I thought you can do anything, God!" However, it's important to remember that the Lord has chosen to work through his people, not independently of them.

He doesn't have to do it this way, but it's the method he has decided to employ. Couldn't he have easily just wiped out Pharaoh and the Egyptians and independently freed the Jews from slavery?

Yes, but he chose to use Moses and Aaron. In the same way, he used men and women throughout the Bible and church history to accomplish his purpose.

Because the Lord wants to use us for his eternal purpose, we must prepare ourselves for use. When instructing Timothy, the Apostle Paul wrote:

> *Therefore, if anyone cleanses himself from what is dishonorable, he will be a vessel for honorable use, set apart as holy, useful to the master of the house, ready for every good work.*
>
> *2 Timothy 2:21 ESV*

Notice that the Lord doesn't cleanse those he calls, he requires those called to cleanse themselves. Just so there's no confusion, this verse is not talking about salvation. No sinner can cleanse themselves of sin.

In context, this passage is speaking to those who are already in Christ and desire to work for the Lord. The sad truth is, not everyone can be used to accomplish the same things for God.

In the verse just before this one, Paul points out that different levels of dedication lead to varying levels of use. God cannot use those who refuse to be set apart.

> *Now in a great house there are not only*
> *vessels of gold and silver but also of*
> *wood and clay, some for honorable use,*
> *some for dishonorable.*
>
> *2 Timothy 2:20 ESV*

It is not God who decides who he can and cannot use; we determine our usefulness (and the level at which God can use us) by our dedication and obedience.

After the Lord told me that I couldn't go any further at that level of prayer, I didn't get angry and discouraged. I began to fast and pray.

I immediately began a twenty-one-day fast, and I called out to God for miracles. My first meeting after that fast ended was in Sussex, New Brunswick, Canada.

One night, after I finished preaching, I announced that I would be laying hands on those who needed a miracle.

There was a woman present who had never been to church before. She answered the altar call to receive Christ and then brought her son, Timothy, to the front of the line to receive prayer.

Timothy, who was six, had been blind in one eye for five years. I felt a compassion come over me that I had never felt. I knew it was the compassion of God. I was reminded of the Scripture:

> *So Jesus had compassion and touched*
> *their eyes. And immediately their eyes*
> *received sight . . .*
>
> *Matthew 20:34 NKJV*

I reached down and hugged the little boy. Laying my hands on his eye, I prayed and asked God to open it by his power. When I removed my hand, the little boy said, "I can see you!"

His mother collapsed to the ground and began to cry as God gave him back his sight.

Since that day, we have witnessed many mighty miracles by the power of the Holy Spirit. Fasting and prayer continue to lead us into supernatural results every single year.

Notice, it wasn't that God wasn't powerful enough to produce miracles before this time. My fasting didn't change God's power; it changed my level of dedication. It set me apart for supernatural use. The same will be true for you.

POWER THAT'S LOCKED IN PRISON

In 1935, the United States completed the most expensive engineering project in its history — the Hoover Dam. The 726-foot, 6.6 million ton wall is still the largest concrete dam in existence.

Every year, Hoover Dam generates enough energy to provide four years of power for a city the size of Dallas, Texas.

The dam holds back the Colorado River and straddles the border of Arizona and Nevada. Behind the dam, Lake Mead is the largest man-made reservoir in the country. There's a lot of water behind that wall.

Now imagine if there were a small hole in the wall. You'd see a stream of water shooting out from the dam. However, it would be a mistake to conclude that there's not much power, or force, behind the dam based on the small stream you see. The only reason the stream seems so insignificant is the size of the dam's hole.

If you were to detonate explosives on the wall, it would burst open, allowing all of the water to come rushing through at once. You'd see true power.

The concrete wall is the only thing standing between you and the full force of the water.

This is an example of how the power of God functions in believers. The dam represents your fleshly, carnal nature, and the water is a picture of the anointing.

It's crucial to understand that you don't need more anointing; you need less of the carnal nature. If you're saved, the Holy Spirit dwells within you. He *is* the anointing of Heaven.

He is the same Spirit that raised Christ from the dead, and now he lives in you (Romans 8:11). If you have a member of the godhead living in your body, you don't need to become more anointed; you need to release the anointing you already have.

THE INTERNAL WAR

It doesn't matter how long you've been saved, the internal war between your flesh and spirit will never end until you die, or your body is glorified in the rapture. The Apostle Paul dealt with this issue in his letter to the Galatians to whom he wrote:

> *For the desires of the flesh are against the Spirit, and the desires of the Spirit are against the flesh, for these are opposed to each other, to keep you from doing the things you want to do.*
>
> *Galatians 5:17 ESV*

Your flesh will never want to do the things that please the Spirit of God. It will continuously fight you. For this reason, you have to take authority over your flesh daily.

Paul wrote to the Corinthian church and explained that he had to control his flesh on a daily basis so that all of his work wouldn't be in vain. He could preach to others and still become disqualified by the end of his life (1 Corinthians 9:27).

Notice how his flesh frustrated him while he was under the Law of Moses:

> *For I do not understand my own actions.*
> *For I do not do what I want, but I do the*
> *very thing I hate.*
> *Romans 7:15 ESV*

He realized that knowing the right thing to do was not enough. We have to be empowered by the Spirit of God to live free from sin. The Holy Spirit gives us power to win every battle against our carnal nature, but we have to take action to subdue our fleshly desires every single day.

BOWING TO YOUR BELLY

The Apostle Paul was very harsh when he dealt with the self-indulgent people who were creeping into the church. Carnally-minded believers brought a flippant attitude to Christianity. As a result, Paul continued to encourage the churches to imitate his way of living.

> *For many, of whom I have often told you*
> *and now tell you even with tears, walk*
> *as enemies of the cross of Christ. Their*
> *end is destruction, their god is their bel-*
> *ly, and they glory in their shame, with*
> *minds set on earthly things.*
> *Philippians 3:18-19 ESV*

Read that phrase again, "their god is their belly." There are carnally-minded Christians who are in danger of becoming enemies of the cross of Christ by living self-indulgent lifestyles.

The reason this is dangerous is that you can become a god unto yourself. It becomes a form of pride that must be dealt with. That's why fasting as a form of self-denial has always been a sign of humility.

You are throwing off the desires of the flesh to pursue the desires of the spirit. Essentially, you're telling the flesh that it's not in control of your decisions. Jesus said it this way:

> *If anyone would come after me, let him*
> *deny himself and take up his cross daily*
> *and follow me.*
> *Luke 9:23 ESV*

Denying your flesh is a significant part of Christianity. As Paul taught, your flesh is working against your spirit. If we will constantly walk by the spirit, we will not fulfill the desires of the flesh (Galatians 5:16).

Walking by the spirit is not only doing the things the Spirit of God wants us to do; it's refusing to do the things the flesh wants to do.

The flesh never wants to seek the Lord in prayer. How often have you begun to pray, and your body quickly becomes tired and your eyes get heavy?

The disciples dealt with the same issue. Their flesh rejected times of prayer. In the Garden of Gethsemane, Jesus found his disciples sleeping after he had called them to pray.

> *And he came to the disciples and found them sleeping. And he said to Peter, "So, could you not watch with me one hour?*
> *Matthew 26:40 ESV*

Jesus spoke of an hour of prayer as though it were minimal. The flesh views an hour of prayer like an impassable mountain.

Jesus was training his disciples to be men of prayer. He didn't just teach them to pray; he modeled a consistent prayer life, knowing that it would transform their ministries as well. Jesus prayed in ways that denied his flesh. He'd pray before sunrise (Mark 1:35), for hours at a time (Matthew 26:39-45), or sometimes through the entire night (Luke 6:12).

This kind of dedicated prayer yielded the power he needed to accomplish the works of his Father. It was a lack of self-denial that kept the disciples from seeing victory in every circumstance.

> *His disciples asked him privately, "Why could we not cast it out?" And he said to them, "This kind cannot be driven out by anything but prayer."*
>
> *Mark 9:28-29 ESV*

A.A. Allen, a mighty tent evangelist during the Voice of Healing movement that took place at the close of World War II, saw many miracles, signs, and wonders in his ministry.

Creative miracles that would blow the natural mind would take place routinely in his revivals. Blind eyes open, cripples walking, cancer healed, deaf ears open, demons cast out, and many more.

As I wrote previously, there was a time when he was very dissatisfied with the results of his ministry. He began to fast and pray. During that time of fasting, Jesus appeared to him and gave him instructions that had to be carried out if he wanted to see miracles happen. You can read this entire story in his book, *The Price of God's Miracle Working Power.*

He relates an experience that took place in the earliest part of his ministry. This experience taught him and his wife about the power of prayer and fasting:

> In one of my early meetings, in southern Missouri, good crowds had been attending for a week, but not one soul had responded to the altar call. My wife and I decided that this *must* be changed, and agreed between ourselves that we would pray all night for souls to be saved in that meeting.
>
> Already we were weary in body, for the hour was late, and the service had been a hard one. Soon weariness began to creep down upon us, and even to stay awake seemed almost impossible.
>
> Again and again, one must waken the other. There was no shouting, no excitement—nothing to keep us awake but the knowledge that in this little community which God had given to us as our responsibility, souls were lost, and we must see them saved. And we had promised God to

pray it through.

As the sun crept over the eastern horizon, we knew that we had kept our vow, and that something was going to happen that night. We could hardly wait for the time of the service.

And that night, victory came. One after another responded to the call, until nineteen souls had found salvation, and were shouting the praises of God in a little country schoolhouse under the ministry of a preacher who had only been preaching three weeks.

As we went home rejoicing from that service, we knew that God had taught us a lesson—it pays to *deny self*.[1]

If we want to be mightily used by God, there can be no excuse. We must deny our flesh and press into the realm of the spirit.

Make up your mind that, unlike the disciples, you will never allow a lack of dedication to hinder you from accomplishing what God called you to do.

Don't just read this book and understand the importance of fasting and prayer; take time to *actually* fast and pray. God will use you to impact your generation for his kingdom before it's too late.

Chapter Three

WHAT IS BIBLICAL FASTING?

Heinrich Friedrich Wilhelm Gesenius, was a gifted German theologian and scholar. He was born in Nordhausen in 1786, and at the age of twenty, he became an adjunct professor.

Four years passed, and he became a *professor extrodinarius* in theology. Just a year later, at the astounding age of twenty-five, he was promoted to *ordinarius* (a professor of the highest rank in a German university) at the University of Halle, where he spent the rest of his life teaching.[1]

He was such a talented orator that his lecture hall was often filled. By the year 1810, his lectures were attended by over 500 students — almost half of the university's student body.[2]

Gesenius had immense influence as a master of the Hebrew language. The editors of the Brown-Driver-Briggs lexicon refer to him as the "father of modern Hebrew Lexicography."[3]

In 1829, Gesenius published his now-famous *Hebrew and Chaldee Lexicon to the Old Testament Scriptures.* Under the section of the Hebrew word *tsowm* (meaning "to fast" as found in 2 Samuel 12:16, etc.), he points out that "the primary idea lies in the mouth being shut."[4]

Therefore, the most literal understanding of the Hebrew word for fasting is *to close or cover the mouth.*

NEW WAVE FASTING

Over the years, I've had many conversations with believers about fasting. It never ceases to amaze me what many consider it to mean.

Some give up donuts or sugar, while others decide to fast watching TV. I've had teenagers tell me that they're fasting social media or video games.

Many modern-day Christians have modified fasting to be whatever they want it to be. In some cases, they've chosen extremely convenient things rather than engaging in true, biblical fasting and prayer.

Obviously, there were no video games or social media in Bible times. Fasting, in context, could not have been referring to entertainment, delicacies, or things we personally enjoy.

While it may be beneficial to give these things up while fasting to seek the Lord more fully, abstaining from them alone is not fasting. Fasting is easy to define. It simply means to not eat.

I agree that during fasting and prayer, we shouldn't be spending our time watching movies and TV, browsing social media, getting lost in YouTube's recommended for you section, or sleeping the fast away. We should use our time wisely to press into God's presence and seek his face.

The problem with these other types of "fasting" is that they don't fully accomplish one of the central purposes of fasting — crucifying the flesh.

Many Christians were controlled by their carnal, fleshly nature long before cell phones, video games, TV, or social media were invented. Paul wrote:

> *For the desires of the flesh are against the Spirit, and the desires of the Spirit are against the flesh, for these are opposed to each other, to keep you from doing the things you want to do.*
>
> *Galatians 5:17 ESV*

God instituted fasting to weaken the flesh as his people were pressing into the spirit realm. Nothing accomplishes that goal more quickly than a lack of calories.

Abstaining from food altogether is the biblical pattern of fasting. It's refusing to allow your flesh to have what it wants. In some instances, Paul allowed married couples to even abstain from sexual intercourse during intense times of prayer.

> *Do not deprive one another [of sex], except perhaps by agreement for a limited time, that you may devote yourselves to prayer; but then come together again, so that Satan may not tempt you because of your lack of self-control.*
> *1 Corinthians 7:5 ESV (Emphasis added)*

While it's not mentioned in this passage, some later Greek manuscripts add the phrase "fasting and prayer" to this verse.[5]

Though whether or not fasting was mentioned is debated, it's clear that Paul was referring to a time of intense devotion to prayer.

The goal is to subdue the carnal, sinful nature and, as Paul wrote, "keep it under control." (See 1 Corinthians 9:27.) Sadly, many Christians allow their flesh to run

WHAT IS BIBLICAL FASTING?

wild, and they're totally out of control. This is dangerous. Paul told the Corinthian believers that this kind of
ongoing lifestyle would lead to disqualification.

It's essential to remember that fasting was not an afterthought for Christ or the first-century believers. As
we cover in other chapters, Jesus expected his followers
to fast and pray. (See Matthew 6:6, 16-18; 9:15)

BIBLICAL FASTING MEANS NO FOOD

Wherever you read about fasting in the Old or New Testament, those who did it ate nothing. (We will explain
the subject of the Daniel Fast in a later chapter.)

Not only did God's people abstain from food, in some
cases, they didn't even drink water.

> *"Go, gather all the Jews to be found in
> Susa, and hold a fast on my behalf, and
> do not eat or drink for three days, night
> or day. I and my young women will also
> fast as you do . . ."*
> **Esther 4:16 ESV**

After his experience on the road to Damascus, Paul
ate and drank nothing for three days (Acts 9:9). Though
some argue that he was in shock rather than fasting for

religious purposes, these are the only two natural total fasts we see in Scripture. Although Moses fasted for forty days and in that time drank nothing, he was obviously supernaturally sustained by God's power.

Moses was in the immediate presence of the Lord for those forty days. As a result, when he descended from the mountain, he had to wear a veil over his face because the glory of God shone so brightly upon him. (See Exodus 34:28.)

Obviously, nobody can go without water for forty days. Abstaining from water for longer than three days can be very damaging to your body.

I never encourage believers to engage in a total fast (no food or water). Unless God's Spirit leads you to close yourself away for one to three days with little to no activity to fast and pray for a serious situation, don't do it. Fasting food is plenty for any believer.

It's all Jesus did. Think about that.

FASTING IS NOT A HUNGER STRIKE

It must be said that fasting by itself is meaningless. God never intended for his people to fast for the sake of fasting. It must *always* be accompanied by prayer.

Think of fasting as a prayer supplement. It's a spiritual discipline that assists you in times of prayer.

Recently, I purchased a pair of blue light glasses because I spend so much time working on digital devices. Supposedly, these glasses block the harmful blue light that comes from phones, tablets, and laptops which delays the body's release of melatonin—the hormone that helps to induce sleep.

When I opened the package, I saw the company had included a test kit to prove that the glasses worked as promised. Inside, I found a blue light laser pointer, a white strip, and the glasses.

The instructions said to shoot the blue light directly onto the white strip. As I did, the blue beam burned a black streak across the bright rectangle proving the harmful nature of the light.

Next, the kit instructed me to place the strip behind one of the lenses and repeat the procedure. This time, the white strip was completely unaffected by the blue beam. The lens had done its job and filtered out the light.

Imagine if God's voice was that blue light. We want the imprint of his voice upon our hearts. However, our flesh is like the filter of the blue light glasses. It's constantly rejecting his voice.

Many believers are so controlled by their flesh that it dominates their lives and minds. Many don't hear clearly from the Holy Spirit (or at all) because their flesh is like a filter that drowns out his voice.

Fasting is the element that removes the "flesh filter" and renews your sensitivity to the Holy Spirit's voice.

If you ever find yourself fasting but not praying, studying, or pressing into God's presence, you should either stop fasting, or begin pressing in.

Bishop David Oyedepo, pastor of one of the world's largest churches in Nigeria, said, "If you're fasting and you're not praying for at least an hour a day, you might as well eat something." I heartily agree with him.

There are many things to which we will give an hour of our time: going out to eat with friends, streaming a show online, shopping, etc.

If we're cutting out food to seek God, an hour of prayer each day is a basic action of dedication to the Lord. In fact, Jesus didn't consider an hour of prayer to be a long time.

> *And he came to the disciples and found*
> *them sleeping. And he said to Peter, "So,*
> *could you not watch with me one hour?*
> *Matthew 26:40 ESV*

The first century believers seemed to have a daily custom of an "hour of prayer" in which they met in the Temple to seek the face of God (Acts 3:1).

Especially during times of fasting, prayer must be paramount in our daily lives. Otherwise, we're only fooling ourselves. There is no power released solely from fasting. If there were, Muslims, Jews, Hindus, Mormons, and Baha'ais would all be walking in miracle power because they fast.

When we fast and pray, we're interacting with the only true and living God — Jehovah.

MAKE A DECISION

I want to encourage you to make up your mind that you're going to be a believer who fulfills Christ's expectation to fast and pray.

Prioritize it and dedicate yourself to seeking the Lord. It's our actions of faith and dedication that prove our spiritual hunger. Many people forget that God promised to reward us for our dedication.

> *Blessed are those who hunger and thirst*
> *for righteousness, For they shall be filled.*
> *Matthew 5:6 NKJV*

The devil cannot withstand believers who fast and pray. As you'll discover in the upcoming chapters, there are many supernatural benefits of fasting and prayer.

Many have taught that humbling your flesh is the only thing accomplished by fasting. You'll quickly learn, however, that isn't the case.

Maybe you've never taken time to fast. It's a good time to start. Don't be intimidated. You don't need to begin with a twenty-one day fast. Nowhere in the Bible are we commanded to fast for any specific length of time.

In *The Patriot*, the film about the American Revolutionary War, Mel Gibson, who plays the lead role of Benjamin Martin, must teach his youngest son to shoot a gun. To help him in the early stages of aiming and shooting a firearm, he teaches him the phrase, "Aim small, miss small."

As an inexperienced shooter, his young son would be ill-advised to attempt headshots or sharpshooting. Aim somewhere that's easier to hit.

That's the same advice I would give someone new to fasting. Don't aim at something large that you've never accomplished before. (e.g. A twenty-one day fast.)

Start small. Maybe give God twenty-four hours of fasting and prayer. From there, move on to three days. Whatever you do, start somewhere, and start immediately. God will bless you for your faith and obedience to his Word.

Always remember, fasting is not, and has never

been optional. If we want to imitate our Master—Jesus Christ—then we must also imitate his dedication and consecration to his heavenly Father.

As you read this book, ask the Lord to guide you by his Spirit in prayer and fasting. He will speak to you and guide the steps of your life. Your best days are ahead.

If we could reproduce Christ's works without duplicating his dedication, we'd be greater than Jesus.

Chapter Four

IS FASTING NECESSARY FOR NEW TESTAMENT BELIEVERS?

I was scrolling through my YouTube notifications one day and saw a comment posted on one of my videos in which I taught on fasting.

The commenter, who obviously disagreed with fasting, wrote, "Fasting is a totally religious tradition! It is not commanded by anyone anywhere after the Old Testament. The New Testament voids all Old Testament traditions."

One of the things he pointed out was that although Jesus mentioned fasting in the Gospel of Matthew, Jesus hadn't yet died, and so, technically, it was still the Old Testament period.

It's not only this commenter who disagrees about the necessity of fasting in the New Testament age; there are

other Christians who don't believe fasting is a requirement for the modern-day believer.

In this chapter, I will explain you why it is the responsibility of every Christian to include fasting with
their prayers as they dedicate themselves to God. Fasting isn't something we should only do once; it's a Christian discipline that should be done regularly.

JESUS IS OUR ROLE MODEL

One of the most important things to remember is that
Christ is our example. In Matthew chapter 10, Jesus
taught his disciples about the persecution that would
come because they were his followers. He was showing
them that what was true for him would become true for
anyone that followed him.

> *A disciple is not above his teacher, nor*
> *a servant above his master. It is enough*
> *for the disciple to be like his teacher, and*
> *the servant like his master.*
> *Matthew 10:24-25 ESV*

Although the context of this passage is referring to
persecution, the principle applies to every area of life.
We are the disciples of Christ. We can never be above

him, nor can we achieve what he achieved without the faithful dedication to God that he modeled.

For example, Christ expects his followers to accomplish the same miraculous things he did when he lived on the earth.

In John chapter 14, Jesus explained that his miraculous works are proof that he was sent by the Father (John 14:10-11). As he did with the Jews in John 10:37-38, he told Philip to believe his confession that he is the Son of God. Otherwise, "believe on account of the works [miracles] themselves."

In the very next verse, Jesus revealed his expectation for his followers — the same works he did.

> *Truly, truly, I say to you, whoever believes in me will also do the works that I do; and greater works than these will he do, because I am going to the Father.*
> *John 14:12 ESV*

We can clearly see that Christ expected his followers to replicate his miraculous works. These miracles were produced not only by his twelve apostles (Acts 5:12) and by the many other disciples of Jesus (Luke 10:17), but continued in the lives of believers after the original apostles died.[1]

If we could reproduce Christ's works without duplicating his example of prayer and fasting, we would certainly be above our master.

We are to be *like* our master. It's fascinating to me that the very first thing Jesus was led to do after being filled with the Spirit was to fast.

It's also worth mentioning that Jesus was truly fasting during his temptation. It wasn't a supernatural encounter like Moses had during his forty days of fasting while in the presence of God (Exodus 34:28).

We know Moses' encounter was supernatural because not only did he fast, he didn't drink water for forty days—a physical impossibility. Unlike Moses' experience, the Bible says Jesus was hungry after he fasted.

> *And Jesus, full of the Holy Spirit, returned from the Jordan and was led by the Spirit in the wilderness for forty days, being tempted by the devil. And he ate nothing during those days. And when they were ended, he was hungry.*
> **Luke 4:1-2 ESV**

Jesus wasn't led to preach the gospel, heal the sick, cast out devils, or raise the dead after his empowerment. He was led to *fast*.

Notice the result of his time of fasting, prayer, and overcoming the devil's temptation in the wilderness.

> *And Jesus returned in the power of the Spirit to Galilee, and a report about him went out through all the surrounding country.*
>
> *Luke 4:14 ESV*

Fasting and prayer prepared Jesus for his earthly ministry, and he is our role model. His fasting and prayer weren't arbitrary.

In Mark chapter 9, his disciples were confused about their inability to cast a demon out of a boy. He explained the problem to them.

> *And he said to them, "This kind cannot be driven out by anything but prayer [and fasting].*
>
> *Mark 9:29 ESV*

Though many modern translations omit the term "and fasting" from this verse, Most manuscripts, even early and excellent ones, have "and fasting" after "prayer" here.[2]

The point that Jesus was making to his disciples was

that the reason for their failure was not their humanity versus his deity, it was their lack of dedication to the Lord.

In many instances (including this one), when the disciples failed to produce supernatural works, Jesus rebuked them. He called them "faithless" (Mark 9:19).

The same thing happened when they failed to calm the sea in Mark chapter 4. It's evident throughout Jesus' ministry that he expected his disciples to replicate his works *and* his dedication to the Father.

When they fell asleep, rather than continuing in extended prayer with him in Gethsemane, he woke them up and rebuked them.

Jesus never referred to a "deity gap" between himself and his followers. He presented himself as the model and example of God's expectation, and then encouraged and anointed them to do what he did.

JESUS EXPECTS HIS FOLLOWERS TO FAST

The content of Jesus' teaching in Matthew chapters 6 and 9 should be enough for any believer to understand that Christ expects his followers to engage in fasting and prayer.

Matthew chapters 5 through 7 give us Jesus' famous Sermon on the Mount. In the sixth chapter, he taught on three specific subjects: giving, prayer, and fasting. While emphasizing each point, he uses the term "when."

When you give (Matthew 6:2), when you pray (Matthew 6:5), and when you fast (Matthew 6:16). Notice that Jesus didn't say, "If you fast." He expected that his followers would fast.

Some may argue that he was teaching a group of Jewish people who were already doing those things in an Old Testament context. However, as I'll show you later in this chapter, as Christ's redemptive work didn't cancel the responsibility of giving or prayer for New Testament believers, neither did it eradicate the necessity of fasting.

What Jesus was correcting was giving, praying, and fasting to be seen by others. It was a form of religious pride that had to be dealt with if there were going to be supernatural blessings for their actions.

Rather than fasting or praying openly to be seen by others, Jesus instructed them to do it privately before the Lord, who would reward them.

> *But when you pray, go into your room and shut the door and pray to your Father who is in secret. And your Father who sees in secret will reward you.*
>
> *Matthew 6:6 ESV*

The Pharisees fasted twice a week to be seen as "extra holy" by those who observed them. Jesus was condemning their hypocrisy and assuring the crowds that sincere actions of sacrifice completed in private humility would be openly commended.

BUT JESUS' DISCIPLES DIDN'T FAST!

Those who may have only scanned through the gospels may be under the impression that Jesus was okay with his apostles abandoning the practice of fasting.

John's disciples questioned Jesus about this in Matthew, chapter 9. "Why do we and the Pharisees fast, but your disciples do not fast?" they asked him.

> *And Jesus said to them, "Can the wedding guests mourn as long as the bridegroom is with them? The days will come when the bridegroom is taken away from them, and then they will fast.*
> *Matthew 9:15 ESV*

Notice Jesus' response—"and then *they will fast.*" Again, this wasn't Jesus saying that it might happen; he was clearly stating his expectation for his followers.

The YouTube commenter I told you about at the beginning of the chapter made the argument that the fasting Jesus was referring to was only between his crucifixion and the Day of Pentecost. It was the commenter's opinion that Jesus returned at Pentecost and ended the fasting requirement.

First, that's not true. Jesus is in Heaven at the right hand of the Father. He won't return until the Rapture and again at his Second Coming.

It was the Holy Spirit who was sent to the believers on the Day of Pentecost as Jesus prophesied.

Secondly, if fasting is merely a religious tradition or a way to attempt to manipulate God into moving, why were the believers still fasting and praying *after* the Day of Pentecost as a means of hearing from the Lord? Look at the example of the early church.

> *While they were worshiping the Lord and fasting, the Holy Spirit said, "Set apart for me Barnabas and Saul for the work to which I have called them." Then after fasting and praying they laid their hands on them and sent them off.*
> *Acts 13:2-3 ESV*

Notice that after their first session of fasting and prayer, instructions came from the Lord to separate Saul and Barnabas into the ministry. However, before taking that action, they fasted and prayed *again* to prepare themselves for the task.

The believers continued to fast and pray as churches were planted, and leaders were commissioned.

> **And when they had appointed elders for them in every church, with prayer and fasting they committed them to the Lord in whom they had believed.**
>
> **Acts 14:23 ESV**

The practice of fasting and prayer not only continued through the New Testament, but also throughout church history.

Somewhere around AD 150, Polycarp, who was a disciple of John the Revelator, wrote to the Philippian church saying:

> ...let us turn back to the word which was delivered to us in the beginning, "watching unto prayer" and persevering in fasting, beseeching the all-seeing God in our supplications "to lead us not into temptation," even as the Lord said, "The spirit is willing, but the flesh is weak."[3]

Thanks to the discovery of the *Didache* (manuscripts that record the extra-biblical teaching of the twelve apostles), we know that the tradition of the Christians in the early church was to fast two days every week — Wednesdays and Fridays.[4]

They chose those days so they wouldn't be fasting on the same days as the Jewish hypocrites (Mondays and Thursdays). The mention of these hypocrites was a reference to what Jesus taught in Matthew chapter 6.

As you can see, Christ's expectation has continued to be fulfilled as his followers have faithfully fasted and prayed throughout the history of the New Testament church.

In the same way that no believer can excuse themselves from the responsibility of giving or prayer, the discipline of fasting must also be present in every Christian's life who desires to please and obey our Lord, Jesus Christ.

So I urge you to imitate me. —Paul the Apostle

Chapter Five

DID THE APOSTLE PAUL BELIEVE IN FASTING?

One of the arguments against fasting that I've encountered is that the Apostle Paul—the most influential man in the New Testament outside of Christ—didn't teach the churches about fasting in his letters, so it must not really be that important for New Testament Christians to fast.

I want to take this chapter to examine Paul's life and ministry and determine whether or not this argument can be substantiated.

First, let's look at the passages of Scripture that deal with Paul and fasting.

Paul was a Pharisee before his conversion. As such, he would have routinely fasted for two days every week. Paul was already accustomed to a life of fasting.

In Acts chapter 9, as Saul is on the road to Damascus, he has an encounter with Jesus and is struck blind. After that interaction, the men traveling with him brought him into Damascus, and the Bible says:

> *And for three days he was without sight,*
> *and neither ate nor drank.*
>
> **Acts 9:9 ESV**

Believe it or not, this is actually a relatively controversial chapter regarding fasting. Not everyone believes that Paul was truly fasting as a form of spiritual dedication.

After he dismisses what is later found in the Didache as an early example of fasting before baptism, British biblical scholar Dr. F.F. Bruce adds that Paul's three days of fasting were "probably the result of shock."[1]

However, not all scholars hold the same opinion. Dr. Darrell L. Bock, Senior Research Professor of New Testament studies at Dallas Theological Seminary, writes, "For three days [Saul] sits in darkness and probably fasts by having no food or drink, processing what has taken place."[2]

Imagine what the Apostle Paul must have felt. He was a profoundly religious man who had dedicated his life to Judaism and spearheaded the newly-established

Christian church's persecution.

Now, after an encounter with Jesus, he realized that he had been actively persecuting the God he meant to serve.

As fasting had been a form of mourning throughout the Old Testament, it's not beyond the scope of imagination that Paul, now convicted about his actions, spent these days in fasting as a form of humbling himself.

In his commentary on the book of Acts, Dr. I. Howard Marshall, Emeritus Professor of New Testament Exegesis at the University of Aberdeen, writes:

> Here [Saul] fasted for three days, no doubt still overcome by shock and probably by penitence as the enormity of his action increasingly dawned upon him.[3]

I think it's safe to assume that Paul was truly humbling himself in fasting and contemplation during these three days before his conversion to Christianity. He certainly continued the habit of fasting after salvation.

RELIGIOUS FASTING OR FORCED HUNGER?

Next, let's look at a few passages in Paul's letters to the Corinthians that some have used to teach on fasting in the context of religious dedication. However, within the context of these three passages, it's easy to see that Paul is talking about the sacrificial price he paid to do the work that an apostle is called to do.

> *But as servants of God we commend our-*
> *selves in every way: by great endurance,*
> *in afflictions, hardships, calamities,*
> *beatings, imprisonments, riots, labors,*
> *sleepless nights, hunger;*
> *2 Corinthians 6:4-5 ESV*

Rather than "hunger," the King James Version uses the term "fastings." However, we can see by the point Paul is making to the church that he isn't referring to fasting and prayer; rather, the things he has endured for Christ's sake. We can read a similar passage later as Paul is "boasting" about his suffering:

> *Are they servants of Christ? I am a better*
> *one—I am talking like a madman—with*
> *far greater labors . . . in toil and hard-*
> *ship, through many a sleepless night, in*
> *hunger and thirst, often without food, in*
> *cold and exposure.*
> *2 Corinthians 11:23,27 ESV*

Clearly, Paul isn't talking about fasting and prayer, but his endurance for Christ. Traveling in AD 55 wasn't as easy or convenient as modern-day travel.

We often take our technological advancements for granted, but we live in a time when life has become very convenient. Paul couldn't reserve a suite at a Hilton or book a flight to another country.

It took extreme dedication to continually travel and complete the work God had assigned to him. But that didn't mean Paul wasn't a man of fasting and prayer.

> *Now there were in the church at Antioch prophets and teachers, Barnabas . . . and Saul. While they were worshiping the Lord and fasting, the Holy Spirit said, "Set apart for me Barnabus and Saul for the work to which I have called them." Then after fasting and praying they laid their hands on them and sent them off.*
> *Acts 13:1-3 ESV*

Before he was set apart into the ministry, we can see Paul fasting with the other Christian leaders in Antioch as he prepared himself for the work of God.

This seems to be the normal practice in the early church. As new churches were being planted, and elders chosen to oversee them, fasting and prayer were common elements of dedication before important decisions were made.

After Paul was stoned in Lystra, he and Barnabas continued to Derbe, Lystra (again), Iconium, and Antioch. After they had made many disciples, it was time to appoint leaders.

> *And when they had appointed elders for them in every church, with prayer and fasting they committed them to the Lord in whom they had believed.*
>
> *Acts 14:23 ESV*

Without question, the Scripture shows us that Paul was a man of fasting and prayer. The question remains, if he believed fasting was important, why didn't he include teaching on the subject of fasting in his letters?

WHY DIDN'T PAUL WRITE ABOUT FASTING?

I've already shown from the Scripture that Paul was a man of fasting. Along with the three passages in the book of Acts that describe his fasting, we can assume that he fasted weekly along with the rest of the believers in the early church.

As I covered in the chapter entitled *Is Fasting Necessary for New Testament Believers*, we have a historical record that the believers fasted for two days every week.

As a deeply religious man who began in the Pharisees' tradition, there is no reason to believe that Paul didn't also engage in this custom with the rest of the believers.

So if he faithfully engaged in fasting, why didn't he write about it? It's important to remember that Paul didn't just write whatever he wanted. All Scripture is inspired (breathed out) by God (2 Timothy 3:16). Remember this important principle:

> *No prophecy of Scripture comes from someone's own interpretation. For no prophecy was ever produced by the will of man, but men spoke from God as they were carried along by the Holy Spirit.*
> *2 Peter 1:20-21 ESV*

Paul was carried along by the Holy Spirit and what he wrote was inspired by God. The Holy Spirit didn't see fit to include any instructions about fasting to the early church. However, that's not an indication that the Holy Spirit didn't want the believers to fast and pray.

There are other fundamental doctrinal principles that

the Holy Spirit didn't inspire Paul to write to the church about. Consider Christ's virgin birth. Paul never wrote once about the virgin birth of Jesus to any of the churches. Do you think that means he didn't believe Jesus was born of a virgin?

Do you think the Holy Spirit didn't think it was an important enough topic to cover? Obviously, Paul believed in the concept of the virgin birth because it's the foundational principle of the gospel message. Paul writes:

> *For I am not ashamed of the gospel, for it is the power of God for salvation to everyone who believes, to the Jew first and also to the Greek.*
>
> *Romans 1:16 ESV*

The gospel to which Paul is referring begins with Jesus being born of a virgin. If he wasn't, he could not have had sinless blood to be shed for the remission of our sins. Without the virgin birth, the entire gospel message becomes meaningless.

Paul, who had access to Luke's gospel, would have been very familiar with the concept of the virgin birth, as would the Christian churches. However, the Holy Spirit didn't feel it necessary to write about it again.

JESUS IS GREATER THAN PAUL

As with the virgin birth, the Holy Spirit didn't inspire Paul to write about fasting, either. There are valid reasons why this is the case.

First, God only has to command his followers to do something once for it to be valid. If he commanded us not to murder in the book of Exodus, he doesn't have to repeat it in every book of the Bible.

When John's followers asked Jesus about his disciples' fasting habits, he said:

> *Can you make wedding guests fast while the bridegroom is with them? The days will come when the bridegroom is taken away from them, and then they will fast in those days.*
>
> *Luke 5:34-35 ESV*

That was Jesus' expectation for his followers. An expectation of Christ is the same as a command. If he said his followers would do something and they didn't do it, are they truly his followers? If his followers refused to fast, does that make Jesus a liar? No. It makes those followers disobedient.

Secondly, we know that Jesus' followers *did* faithfully

fast every week. It was the common practice of every believer in the early church. It would stand to reason that if everyone is obediently engaged in the discipline of fasting, you don't need to command them to fast.

Therefore, it would have been unnecessary to write to the believers about fasting if it was commonly practiced.

We can conclude from his own personal dedication to fasting that Paul believed in the practice, and modeled it for the believers in the early church.

In fact, knowing that he was a man of fasting, we might even say that he did encourage the believers to fast—albeit indirectly.

> *I urge you, then, be imitators of me. That is why I sent you Timothy, my beloved and faithful child in the Lord, to remind you of my ways in Christ, as I teach them everywhere in every church.*
>
> ***1 Corinthians 4:16-17 ESV***

It's interesting to me how this passage is worded. Paul sent Timothy to the church to remind them of his "ways in Christ." Ways that he taught everywhere in every church.

As Paul was a man of fasting and prayer, he would

have taught these principles to all new believers and encouraged them to do the same faithfully. He reiterates this sentiment later in his letter, probably because of its importance for those being discipled to have a human example to follow.

>*Be imitators of me, as I am of Christ.*
>   *1 Corinthians 11:1 ESV*

Go and gather together all the Jews and fast for me. Do not eat or drink for three days.
—Esther

Chapter Six

HOW LONG SHOULD I FAST AND PRAY?

One of the questions I'm asked most often when teaching on fasting and prayer is, "How long should I fast?" This is a problematic question for a few reasons.

First, the Scripture doesn't give us any commands about how long or how often we should fast. Since we have no command, we can only look at examples throughout the biblical narrative.

Second, one attribute that should define New Testament believers is that God's Spirit leads them. Everyone is different and must hear God's voice for themselves.

> *For all who are led by the Spirit of God*
> *are sons of God.*
>
> *Romans 8:14 ESV*

Third, we could set unbiblical expectations for individual fasting (I'll talk about corporate fasting later) by falling into the trap of comparison.

You may think, *Pastor Chris fasted for twenty-one days. I'm going to do the same!* That's a terrible reason to begin a fast. God may have led Pastor Chris to fast for twenty-one days because of what's taking place in his purpose.

> **But when they measure themselves by one another and compare themselves with one another, they are without understanding.**
>
> **2 Corinthians 10:12 ESV**

The phrase "they are without understanding" could also be translated, "they are unintelligent."[1] It's unwise to compare yourself to someone else in this way. You could just as easily say, "Pastor Dennis doesn't fast. I'm not going to fast either."

That comparison would also be foolish because we know that fasting is an expectation of Christ. Comparison is dangerous.

I've heard it said that Pastor Enoch Adeboye, the General Overseer of the Redeemed Christian Church of God in Nigeria, completed three forty-day fasts every year until he was about seventy years old.

Without question, I believe that's something the Lord led him to do. When you see the extreme fruitfulness of his ministry (many times under heavy resistance) and the worldwide effects of his spiritual leadership, you'd be a fool to doubt it.

Do I believe this is a model for every Christian? Absolutely not. I believe what the Lord has called you to do determines the depth of your preparation and dedication in this area.

I realize that may be a controversial thought. Remember, however, that although we have record of Jesus fasting for forty days, we have no biblical account of the Apostle Paul (arguably the most effective apostle in Scripture) fasting for longer than three days.

It makes sense that an individual who is called by God to full-time ministry may do something different than the average believer.

For example, although I have a daily workout regimen for my physical health, I don't work out in the same way that a professional athlete would. It's their job to be in peak physical condition, whereas I'm only doing it to maintain good health.

The same is true for spiritual leaders. Their call is to be in peak spiritual condition for the perfecting of the saints (Ephesians 4:12), while the believer is staying in strong spiritual health as they live for Christ.

Undoubtedly, every believer should engage in ongoing fasting and prayer, but the frequency and length will differ as they are individually led. It will also probably differ from those who are called into full-time ministry.

BIBLICAL FASTS BY LENGTH

Now that you understand that although we're expected to fast and pray and there's no biblically-prescribed length, I want to walk you through the lengths of fasts we can see modeled in the Bible.

Sunrise to Sunset Fast

The shortest length of a fast that we can see modeled in Scripture is what may be commonly called the "six to six fast." You may have heard me encourage those who join us for extended fasts to fast from 6 a.m. to 6 p.m.

I've heard people criticize this fast saying that Christians are "fasting like Muslims." (Muslims commonly fast this way during Ramadan — their month of sacrifice and prayer.)

However, anyone with even a cursory knowledge of history knows that Islam wasn't founded until the 7th century. God's people had modeled this type of fasting well over 1,500 years before.

In Judges chapter 20, the tribes of Israel had engaged

the tribe of Benjamin in two separate battles and lost on both occasions. The death toll was already above 40,000 men from Israel.

Israel fasted and prayed until sunset while asking the Lord for guidance. Afterward, he promised that they would defeat the tribe of Benjamin. The next day, they won the battle and ended the conflict as the Lord said they would.

> *Then all the people of Israel, the whole army, went up and came to Bethel and wept. They sat there before the LORD and fasted that day until evening, and offered burnt offerings and peace offerings before the LORD.*
>
> *Judges 20:26 ESV*

In 2 Samuel 1:12, David's men also fasted until sunset when they heard the terrible news about David's son.

In 1 Samuel 14, Saul commanded his army not to eat before evening until the Philistines were defeated.

Rather than engaging in a "Daniel Fast," to which I've dedicated an entire chapter, I suggest those who are new to fasting begin with this type of a "six to six" fast before advancing to longer fasts.

Use that time to faithfully seek the Lord in prayer and

study of his Word. This will be far more beneficial than an extended diet that doesn't crucify the flesh.

24-Hour Fast

Next, we see a full, twenty-four hour fast modeled in Scripture. The Pharisees boasted about the fact that they fasted two days every week.

> *I fast twice a week; I give tithes of all that I get.*
> *Luke 18:12 ESV*

Although the Pharisees fasted two days each week, they weren't consecutive days. They were two, twenty-four hour fasts each week that historically took place on Mondays and Thursdays.

Once, when teaching his disciples, Jesus pointed to the dedication of the Pharisees and said:

> *For I tell you, unless your righteousness exceeds that of the scribes and Pharisees, you will never enter the kingdom of heaven.*
> *Matthew 5:20 ESV*

Obviously, those in the kingdom of God shouldn't be less dedicated than the religious leaders who were living under an old covenant.

This is why the disciples also fasted two days a week. As I previously wrote, the *Didache* confirms that Christians in the first century were fasting on Wednesdays and Fridays as to not be fasting simultaneously with the "hypocrites."

In the Old Testament, Israel also fasted for an entire day for the purpose of repentance. The prophet Samuel prayed, offered a sacrifice, and God delivered them from the Philistines. (See 1 Samuel 7:5-11.)

A 24-hour fast is clearly modeled in Scripture (and throughout church history) and is also a great starting point for anyone who is just getting involved with fasting and prayer.

3-Day Fast

In the book of Esther, Mordecai—Queen Esther's older cousin—uncovered a plot by the Persian official, Haman, to eradicate the Jewish minority population as an act of revenge.

Mordecai, the Jews, Queen Esther, and her handmaidens fasted food and drink for three full days before she approached King Xerxes for help. God granted their request, and Esther saved the Jewish people.

This fast is unique because the Jews abstained from food *and* drink during these three days.

Other than Moses' supernatural experience of not eating or drinking for forty days, this is the longest example we have in the Bible of a total fast (no solids or liquids).

Although the same type of three-day fast could be attributed to the Apostle Paul after his encounter with Christ on the road to Damascus, I have dedicated the previous chapter to discuss fasting in Paul's life with more in-depth commentary.

Though I wouldn't recommend that believers engage in a total fast (especially with a work schedule), if you do, you shouldn't do so for longer than three days as it can be extremely detrimental to your health.

Remember, the Jews in Esther's day were facing total extermination as a race. They were literally fasting and praying for their lives. Again, I would point you toward the life of Christ. He fasted only food while in the wilderness.

Remember, fasting already heavily subdues your flesh. Your focus should be more on prayer and God's Word than how harshly you can treat your body.

7-Day Fast

At the end of King Saul's reign, Israel was fighting against the Philistines. The men of Israel were slain on Mount Gilboa. All of Saul's sons were killed, and Saul was heavily wounded by the Philistine archers. Saul fell upon his own sword along with his armor-bearer and ended his life.

The Philistines found his body, cut off his head, and stripped his armor. They put his armor in their temple and fastened his body to the wall of Beth-shan — a town overlooking the Jordan valley.

When the men of Jabesh-gilead heard what had happened, they traveled through the night, took Saul and his sons' bodies, and burned them in Jabesh.

Then, in mourning, they fasted for seven days. (See 1 Samuel 31:1-13.)

King David spent seven days fasting and praying for his terminally-ill son in 2 Samuel chapter 12. As soon as the seven days ended, he arose, anointed himself, and ate with his men.

14-Day Fast

There is no true fourteen-day fast in Scripture. When Paul was being taken to Rome, a heavy storm overtook the ship. In anxiety (and probably constant work to save the ship), the crew didn't eat for fourteen days (Acts 27:33).

Note that these men weren't Christians and were not seeking God in fasting and prayer. Most likely, they were too afraid and busy to eat. Paul finally encouraged them to eat something. Paul didn't fast during those fourteen days. When encouraging the crew to eat, he says "it has been fourteen days since 'you' (not 'we') have been without food" (Acts 27:33).

In fact, Paul already knew by revelation of the Spirit that no lives would be lost due to the storm. Thus, he had his answer and did not need to fast (Acts 27:22, 34).

21-Day Fast

As with the fourteen-day fast, there is no true twenty-one-day fast in Scripture. Many have participated in what's commonly known as a "Daniel Fast" for twenty-one days. I cover this topic in-depth in this book in the chapter entitled *The Danger of the Daniel Fast*.

We often begin each year with twenty-one or thirty days of fasting as an act of faith to start the year in dedication, not because the Bible commands it.

40-Day Fast

Finally, we have record of a few forty-day fasts in the Bible. Let's examine each one closely.

As I previously wrote, Moses fasted in the presence of God. In those forty days, he neither ate nor drank anything. We can assume that this fast was a supernatural experience rather than an act of discipline. Obviously, to go without water for forty days is impossible.

I wouldn't consider Moses' fast a true time of fasting. Some add that Joshua fasted along with Moses, but the Bible does not clearly say so.

Secondly, Elijah fasted for forty days after eating what we can identify as a supernatural meal. As he was fleeing Jezebel's murderous rage, he came to the wilderness outside of Beersheba and fell asleep under a tree.

An angel woke him up and provided two meals for him. He ate and drank and those supernatural meals empowered him to complete a forty-day journey to Horeb where God spoke to him.

Again, this wasn't a true fast as he was sustained by supernatural food, and unlike Jesus, the Bible doesn't say he was hungry afterward.

Finally, Jesus truly fasted for forty days and was hungry at the end. Interestingly, each of these men represents different important periods in the Bible and the three important sections of Scripture.

Moses represents the Law, Elijah represents the Prophets, and Jesus represents the New Testament. Jesus referred to these divisions of Scripture.

> *On these two commandments depend all*
> *the Law and the Prophets.*
> *Matthew 24:40 ESV*

Jesus was teaching that the New Testament commands of love fulfill all of the Old Testament teachings.

A forty-day fast is a serious commitment. I believe it's significant that only our Lord Jesus Christ truly engaged in this type of dedication. I would never discourage anyone from fasting, but I would advise anyone who was considering a forty-day fast to consider that choice prayerfully. It's not something to do flippantly. Are you willing and able to take forty days to truly focus on prayer and the Word of God? If you feel led to fast for forty days, by all means, obey the voice of God.

Unspecified Lengths

Throughout the Bible, we have examples of people fasting, but the Scripture doesn't list the length of their dedication to the Lord.

For example, Antioch's prophets and teachers were engaged in fasting and prayer for an unknown time before separating Paul and Barnabas into the ministry (Acts 13:2-3).

Again, after prayer and fasting, Paul and Barnabas appointed elders to the churches (Acts 14:23).

As you'll read in other chapters, I have fasted for different lengths throughout my life as God led me. For example, I fasted for three days before beginning my relationship with Carolyn, I fasted for one day before deciding which college to attend, and I usually begin each year with twenty-one days of fasting.

Sometimes God will lead you to fast for a certain number of days. Other times, you may set a length of time to dedicate yourself to the Lord, and sometimes you may fast until you receive the answer you desire from the Holy Spirit.

It's important to remember that there is no biblical command regarding the length of our fasts. As believers, we must be led by the Spirit of God. Never become legalistic in the length of your fasting. Do it humbly as unto the Lord. He will bless you publicly.

If you're not specific with your prayer requests, you won't recognize your answers.

Chapter Seven

HOW SHOULD I PRAY WHEN I FAST?

When I was in high school, we had student-led prayer before the first bell every morning. Mr. Gripper, one of the science teachers and a member of our church, would allow us to gather in his classroom to begin our days by talking to the Lord.

It was encouraging to see students who had a desire to seek the face of God when they could have been hanging out with their friends in the gym.

Mr. Gripper also sponsored our Bible club, which was one of the most attended clubs with over one hundred members. That's a breakthrough in a public high school.

Although I was happy to be a part of morning prayer, something constantly annoyed me. Before praying, we would go around the room and take everyone's prayer request. Every morning, without fail, there were three sisters who would count and report how many "unspoken" prayer requests they had.

If you didn't grow up in church, you might not be familiar with the "unspoken prayer request." It's basically a religious way of saying that you didn't want the church to know why you needed prayer. Presumably, caused by an embarrassing situation or an extremely personal matter.

It was a common occurrence in our school prayer meeting. Every time the girls tallied and reported their unspoken prayer requests, however, I would feel an irritation but couldn't explain why.

Finally, as I was reading my Bible one day, I discovered why it annoyed my spirit. As I was studying Paul's letter to the Philippians, I saw this verse in a new light:

> *Do not be anxious about anything, but in everything by prayer and supplication with thanksgiving let your requests be made known to God.*
>
> *Philippians 4:6 ESV*

That phrase jumped off of the page at me. Let your requests *be made known* unto God. Unspoken prayer requests aren't scriptural. They're just a way to obscure your requests and keep you from receiving answers to prayer. You can still guard your dignity while expressing a specific need in prayer. For example, you don't have to explain the exact details of what's happening with your body, but if others are going to agree with you in prayer, they need to know they're praying for your healing.

BE SPECIFIC IN PRAYER

Our prayers should always be based upon God's Word. It's a prerequisite to answered prayer. Jesus taught this in John's gospel:

> *If you abide in me, and my words abide*
> *in you, ask whatever you wish, and it*
> *will be done for you.*
> **John 15:7 ESV**

We petition God based upon his Word, because we have a covenant with him based upon his promises. He must do what he has promised, and he cannot lie (Numbers 23:19).

God is always watching over his Word to perform it (Jeremiah 1:12), and when it's released, it will always accomplish what he sends it to do (Isaiah 55:11).

For these reasons, we always base our prayers on God's Word. When I provide prayer points (written prayer goals and requests) to my friends and partners, I provide a Scripture reference next to each one.

This ensures we're asking God for something that he has promised and spoken and not just something we desire because of our carnal nature.

Specificity in prayer also gives us a clear definition of what the answer to our prayers will be. Recently, I was teaching someone the concept of S.M.A.R.T. goals. You may be familiar with this acronym.

If you want to accomplish your goals or create truly effective ones, adding these parameters will be of inestimable value.

The acronym S.M.A.R.T. stands for specific, measurable, achievable, relevant, and time-sensitive. The argument in favor of S.M.A.R.T. goals is that if your goal isn't specific, how would you know you've accomplished it? If it's not measurable, how will you track progress? If it's not realistically achievable, you're planning for frustration. If it's not relevant to your purpose, you're wasting time. Finally, if it's not time-sensitive, you could leave your goals in limbo or take fifteen years to accomplish something that could be done in six months.

Apply this kind of thinking to your prayer life. If you aren't praying specific prayers as the Bible commands, how would you know if God answered your prayers? For example, the prayer request "Bless me, Lord" isn't very productive.

First of all, "blessing" is a relative term. It varies from person to person. What one may consider a blessing could be the status quo to someone else. How would you know if God blessed you?

Instead, be specific. Are you believing for a new job? What kind of job do you want? Praying for healing? Be specific about your desired outcome.

Don't be double-minded regarding healing prayers. Don't say, "Lord heal me of this cancer, but if you won't, anoint the doctor as he cuts the tumor out of my body. But God if you're allowing me to go through this trial for a greater purpose, just give me the strength to endure this for my greater good."

Hopefully, you can see that those three prayer goals are not in any way the same. The last two are unscriptural and won't bring an answer from God.

> *For the one who doubts is like a wave of the sea . . . For that person must not suppose that he will receive anything from the Lord; he is a double-minded man, unstable in all his ways.*
>
> *James 1:6-8 ESV*

When we pray, we must be specific and focused on a single goal. That's what faith does. Make sure that when you're fasting and praying, you set specific goals and write them down. Then, you'll recognize when God answers your specific request.

A THANKSGIVING AND PRAISE SANDWICH

One of the mistakes believers often make is failing to thank and praise God during times of prayer. Thanksgiving and praise are supernatural transactions that provoke God's interaction.

We shouldn't just launch into asking God for things and providing him with our "wish list." We must observe God's order when we approach him.

> *Enter his gates with thanksgiving, and his courts with praise! Give thanks to him; bless his name!*
>
> *Psalm 100:4 ESV*

Imagine if God was on the earth in bodily form seated on a throne. Can you envision yourself simply bursting into the throne room and launching into your demands and desires? I can't.

We must observe God's order. We begin with thanksgiving and continue with praise. I made a rule of thumb for myself, which I've referred to as a thanksgiving and praise sandwich.

Let's say I allotted myself an hour for prayer. I would take the first fifteen minutes to only thank and praise God for what he has *already* done and the promises of his Word.

Only after I've sufficiently thanked and praised him do I begin to make my requests. I'll take the next thirty minutes to stand on Scripture and ask God to move in my life, family, and ministry.

Finally, I'll take the last fifteen minutes to thank and praise him again. Only this time, I'm thanking and praising him for what he's *going* to do, not what he's already done.

I sandwich my requests between two sessions of thanksgiving and praise. It not only ensures I've observed the biblical order of approaching God, it gives me access to the supernatural power that accompanies those two dynamic elements.

The Psalmist wrote that "God inhabits the praises of Israel" (Psalm 22:3). Praise is the quickest access into the presence of the Lord.

I explain the supernatural effects and benefits of praise and thanksgiving in great detail in my book, *Unhang Your Harp.*

You may be surprised to find many of your prayers answered as you take time to praise and thank God. Look what happened for God's people as they praised him:

> *Now when they began to sing and to praise, the LORD set ambushes against the people of Ammon, Moab, and Mount Seir, who had come against Judah; and they were defeated.*
>
> *2 Chronicles 20:22 NKJV*

In the same way that God fought Israel's battle for them as they praised him while marching toward their enemies, God will move on your behalf as you praise and thank him.

THE BENEFITS OF A KINGDOM-FIRST MINDSET

Recently, I was listening to a marketing consultant teach about how to create more successful and productive relationships.

He established something that he calls "The 51/49 Principle" and encourages others to employ it in their lives as well.

The principle's goal is to provide fifty-one percent

of the value in any given relationship while only taking forty-nine percent for yourself. He believes that this makes you a desirable commodity in the business community and will keep people coming back to you to continue the business relationship.

If you think about it, this is simply a spirit of generosity. It's a clear picture of the law of seedtime and harvest in action. The Golden Rule—doing unto others as you would have them do unto you—is simply a seed you're sowing that produces a harvest of generosity.

It's a principle that should be present in prayer. One of the biggest mistakes we could make in prayer is being too self-centered. We must strive for a kingdom mindset in prayer. Remember that God has a plan that he wants to carry out using the body of Christ.

If you put others and the kingdom of God first in prayer, I believe that God will fulfill your personal requests before you have a chance to pray for them. God did this for Job as he prayed for his friends when he could easily have been praying for himself:

> *And the LORD restored the fortunes of Job, when he had prayed for his friends. And the LORD gave Job twice as much as he had before.*
>
> *Job 42:10 ESV*

It's not that God doesn't want to hear your requests; as I've shown you, the Bible commands us to make our requests known unto him. Instead, it's about putting God and his desires first in your life. Whoever puts God first will never finish last. Jesus told us to live this way.

> *But seek first the kingdom of God and his righteousness, and all these things will be added to you.*
> *Matthew 6:33 ESV*

The Lord knows what we need. As we carry out his plans and obey his voice, he will meet our needs and answer our prayers.

Many Christians never move beyond making personal requests to praying kingdom agenda prayers. What is a kingdom agenda prayer? It's a prayer that focuses on God's desires in the earth.

For example, we might say, "Lord, I pray that you would strengthen your ministers around the world in this upcoming year. Give them a renewed boldness as they preach the gospel (Ephesians 6:19). Arise in our nation and supernaturally scatter the plans of the wicked that have been made against your righteous people (Psalm 68:1). As we can see that the harvest is ripe and ready to be reaped, send laborers into your harvest field, and let souls be saved unprecedented numbers this year (Matthew 9:38).

All three of these prayers would be considered kingdom prayers as they express God's plan for the earth. Notice that I also included the Scripture references that I'm standing on to see the fulfillment of each prayer that I pray.

Again, Jesus taught that all the things you need will be added unto you as you seek the kingdom. If you put God's desires first, you'll never have to worry about your desires.

ALIGN YOURSELF WITH GOD'S PERFECT WILL

In February of 2003, I was in Tulsa, Oklahoma, attending Reverend Kenneth Hagin's Winter Bible Seminar. I had been out of Bible school for less than a year, and I was fasting and praying for direction in my life and ministry.

I had known that I was called to be an evangelist since the Lord spoke to me in a little church in New Brunswick, Canada, when I was five years old.

Now, as a twenty-year-old Bible school graduate, I'd begun traveling and had been holding meetings for the last eight months.

As the new year started, I was hungry to hear fresh

direction for my evangelistic ministry, and so I spent time in fasting and prayer.

As I was seeking the Lord, he gave me a word that confused my natural mind. My uncle, Pastor Terry Shuttlesworth, had recently launched Dominion Christian Center in Virginia Beach, Virginia.

The Lord instructed me to stop traveling, move to Virginia, and assist my uncle as he planted that brand-new church.

"I thought you called me to be an evangelist," I prayed to the Lord. "I'm not a pastor." This direction seemed odd to my natural mind, however, I felt peace in my spirit about the decision.

For those being led by the Spirit of God, peace is a spiritual marker that you're moving in the right direction. Joy propels us and peace leads us forward (Isaiah 55:12).

Though I didn't understand the direction at the time, I obeyed the voice of the Lord. Just a few months later, I was living in Virginia and working at the church. Looking back, I can see all of the supernatural things the Lord did for me because of my obedience.

However, to make these types of decisions and overcome the desires or understanding of your flesh, you must be willing to pray prayers of consecration to the Lord.

This is something Jesus modeled for his disciples and New Testament believers when he prayed in the garden of Gethsemane.

Interestingly, Gethsemane is "the place of crushing." It was an oil press where olives were crushed. In messianic prophecy, Isaiah writes:

> *Yet it was the will of the LORD to crush*
> *him; he has put him to grief . . .*
> *Isaiah 53:10 ESV*

Of course, Isaiah was writing about the future Messiah's crucifixion. However, before Jesus' body could be crushed on the cross, his will had to be crushed in the garden. He had to consecrate himself. Jesus prayed:

> *My Father, if it be possible, let this cup*
> *pass from me; nevertheless, not as I will,*
> *but as you will . . . if this cannot pass un-*
> *less I drink it, your will be done.*
> *Matthew 26:39, 42 ESV*

The greatest act of humility you can take is denying your will and obeying God's instructions to carry out his purposes. As fasting is an act of humbling yourself, one of the types of prayer you should pray is the prayer of consecration. To consecrate simply means to formally dedicate something or someone to a divine purpose. That's what we're doing when we pray this way.

We used to sing songs of consecration that were just musical prayers surrendering our will to the Lord. I remember one such song we sang often:

> *I'll say yes, Lord, yes to your will and to your way.*
> *I'll say yes, Lord, yes, I will trust you and obey.*
> *When your spirit speaks to me,*
> *with my whole heart, I'll agree.*
> *My answer will be yes, Lord, yes.*

There's nothing greater than being in God's will for your life. If we're not involved in doing what God is actively doing, we're working in vain (Psalm 127:1).

Take a significant amount of time as you fast and pray to consecrate and dedicate yourself to the Lord, and he will lift you up and show himself strong and mighty on your behalf (2 Chronicles 16:9).

PRAY FOR THOSE IN AUTHORITY

We're also commanded to pray for those in authority. This means those in natural and spiritual authority.

If you aren't dedicating time to pray for your pastor

and his family, begin today. Your pastor is engaged in spiritual warfare for those whom God has given him. People in the community may attack him for the stand he has taken for faith.

The enemy is undoubtedly attempting to attack him because of what he's doing for the Lord. Every responsible believer should be praying for their pastor and his family.

> *For we do not wrestle against flesh and blood, but against the rulers, against the authorities, against the cosmic powers over this present darkness, against the spiritual forces of evil in the heavenly places.*
>
> *Ephesians 6:12 ESV*

Secondly, we should pray for those in leadership positions in our nation. In the United States, pray for your President; in Canada, pray for your Prime Minister, and so on.

Politics can be one of the biggest issues of contention among believers. One of the most disappointing things to hear a believer say when being encouraged to pray for the President is, "He's not *my* President."

Even if you didn't vote for your current political leader (if you live in a democracy), that's not an excuse to refuse to pray for them, or worse, hope that something negative happens to them. Scripture commands believers to pray for those in political leadership.

> *First of all, then, I urge that supplications, prayers, intercessions, and thanksgivings be made for all people, for kings and all who are in high positions, that we may lead a peaceful and quiet life, godly and dignified in every way.*
> *1 Timothy 2:1-2 ESV*

God is pleased when we do this because he wants all people to come to salvation and the knowledge of the truth (1 Timothy 2:3).

I've heard people speak so negatively of their political leaders. "He could never be saved," I've heard some say. Don't you think it's absurd that we believe God can raise the dead and open blind eyes but he can't change a political leader's heart? Pray for those leading your nation, and believe God for revival.

PRAY FOR WISDOM

One of the most vital requests you could ever make to God is to ask for wisdom. It is by far the greatest element in the life of every believer. Wisdom opens the door to many of the other blessings that God has for his people. They follow wisdom automatically.

Solomon, David's son, loved the Lord and walked by his father's example. Once, as he was sacrificing to the Lord at Gibeon, the Lord appeared to him.

"Ask what I shall give you," the Lord said. He asked God for wisdom and understanding. Solomon's answer so pleased God that God not only gave him greater wisdom than anyone has ever had, he also gave him the things for which he *could* have asked.

> *I give you also what you have not asked,*
> *both riches and honor, so that no other*
> *king shall compare with you, all your*
> *days. And if you will walk in my ways . .*
> *. then I will lengthen your days.*
> *1 Kings 3:13-14 ESV*

Wisdom is such a powerful tool because it continually exalts you to higher places. Even if you stripped everything from someone with wisdom, before long, they would have it again — and more.

If you aren't currently wise, Scripture commands you to ask God for wisdom. He won't rebuke you for asking (James 1:5).

Tim Thomason founded Nature Blinds, a company

that makes hunting blinds look so much like real tree stumps that deer will rub against them while the hunter is sitting inside.

One day he prayed, "God, give me a good idea." He heard an audible voice say, "Build a tree."

He went into his garage, where he had foam cutting tools, and began carving a tree. He called the patent office and asked for a patent on trees and rocks. They laughed at him.

Six months later, they called him back to let him know they would grant his patent, and they apologized for laughing at him. It was an idea from God.

He was only fabricating two trees a day and needed a miracle to grow. He finally told the Lord that he needed a divine intervention within twenty-four hours.

He walked out the back door, and there stood a man in flip flops and shorts, who, according to Tim, looked like Shaggy from Scooby-Doo.

"Can I help you?" Thomason asked.

"Yeah," said the man. "I heard about your product, and I wanted to come by and check it out."

After that meeting, Shaggy pulled out a checkbook and wrote Tim a check that financed a brand-new, 50,000 square foot manufacturing plant.

Nature Blinds has become a well-known name in the hunting world, and it made Tim a very wealthy man.

He has since launched the Blind Faith Foundation. They practically show the love of God and are a blessing to those in need through random acts of kindness.[1]

The wisdom of God made it all possible. It all began with one simple prayer — *God, give me a good idea.*

This is a perfect illustration of what the Bible says takes place when someone operates in godly wisdom. Solomon outlines the benefits of finding wisdom:

> *Blessed is the one who finds wisdom . . .*
> *Long life is in her right hand; in her left*
> *hand are riches and honor. Her ways are*
> *ways of pleasantness, and all her paths*
> *are peace.*
>
> *Proverbs 3:13, 16-17 ESV*

There is nothing higher than God's wisdom. His thoughts are higher than our thoughts, and his ways are higher than ours (Isaiah 55:9). However, that's the wonderful thing about having access to his wisdom — we upgrade from finite to infinite.

Unbelievers cannot understand spiritual things (let alone gain access to the wisdom of God), but we have the mind of Christ (1 Corinthians 2:16). We have to be aware of that fact and depend on it continually.

> *Wisdom is supreme—so acquire wis-*
> *dom, and whatever you acquire, acquire*
> *understanding!*
>
> *Proverbs 4:7 NET*

Don't trust in human understanding; depend on the Lord in everything you do, and he will direct your paths. (Proverbs 3:5-6). God's wisdom is the highest element for which we can strive.

BE LED BY THE SPIRIT IN PRAYER

Of course, I can't cover every single thing you should pray during times of fasting. Many things will be personal and apply to your specific situation.

However, I do want to encourage you in one other area. Set a goal to be led by God's Spirit in prayer. During fasting, your flesh will be subdued, and hearing God's voice will be easier than ever.

The Lord will lead you to pray for things you may not know about. Be sensitive to his leading. Remember, prayer is not a monologue; it's a dialogue. The most important part of prayer is not what we say to God; it's what God says to us.

Even when you don't know what or how to pray, the Holy Spirit intercedes for you (Romans 8:26). The ability to be led by the Lord is an invaluable tool that can keep us in constant victory. We must never forget that being led by God's Spirit isn't just a benefit that's available to his children. It's a defining characteristic of the New Testament believer.

> *For all who are led by the Spirit of God are sons of God.*
>
> ***Romans 8:14 ESV***

As the voice of the Lord leads you, expect to see expedited answers to your prayers. After all, quick answers are what God promised when his people engage in the fast that he has chosen. (See Isaiah 58:9.)

I believe that as you fast and pray, you will be filled with joy when you experience the answers to prayer for which you've been believing.

Approach God boldly. Approach him humbly. Approach him daily.

For the spirit is willing, but the body is weak!
—Jesus

Chapter Eight

THE FOUR APPETITES THAT MUST BE DEALT WITH

Sir Arthur Conan Doyle created one of the most well known fictional characters in history — Sherlock Holmes, the world-famous detective. Holmes' cases were chronicled, and his stories were told from the perspective of his best friend and roommate, John Watson, a retired military doctor.

In the first novel Conan Doyle wrote, *A Study in Scarlet*, Dr. Watson meets Holmes for the first time and learns about his astonishing intellect.

Holmes knew many things about various subjects. However, Watson also observed, "His ignorance was as remarkable as his knowledge."

Holmes knew little about literature, philosophy, and politics. Dr. Watson's amazement reached its climax when he realized that Holmes knew nothing of the Copernican Theory and the Solar System's composition. How could anyone not know that the earth rotates around the sun?

"You appear to be astonished," Holmes said. "Now that I do know it, I shall do my best to forget it."

"To forget it!" Watson was incredulous. Holmes explained his train of thought:

> "You see," he explained, "I consider that a man's brain originally is like a little empty attic, and you have to stock it with such furniture as you choose. A fool takes in all the lumber of every sort that he comes across, so that the knowledge which might be useful to him gets crowded out, or at best is jumbled up with a lot of other things, so that he has a difficulty in laying his hands upon it.[1]

Although Sherlock Holmes is a fictional character, Conan Doyle based his extraordinary deductive reasoning on Dr. Joseph Bell, one of his medical school professors at the University of Edinburgh, who exhibited the same deductive talents.

Holmes' explanation of how he prepared his mind to stay in its constant problem-solving state is an example of self-control's vital importance.

If he didn't control what was in his mind, it would be crowded with things that would not only hinder him from accomplishing his goals but render his previously-acquired knowledge useless.

He became an extraordinary detective because he used self-control to organize and gain access to the thoughts that pertained most to his work.

In my estimation, self-control is the most important of the nine Fruit of the Spirit. It keeps your life in divine order rather than descending into chaos.

It would be beneficial at this point to observe the second law of thermodynamics—entropy. Entropy just means *a gradual decline into disorder.*

The Law of Entropy states that isolated systems spontaneously evolve towards total disorder.

In other words, any system left to its own devices will end in chaos, not order. For example, if you went to the beach and built a sandcastle on the shore, when you returned the next day, the quality of the sandcastle would have diminished, not increased.

The wind, the tides, and other forces would interfere with the order of the sandcastle you built and destroy the details you designed.

If there's not an external force maintaining control, chaos will ensue. This principle is what we're dealing with in this chapter.

Your carnal nature not only has desires that are contrary to God's desires, but it will actively pursue them and end in disorder unless you take control.

Through fasting and prayer, we have the ability to conquer carnal desires and surrender ourselves to God's will.

As I've said many times before, if you're not prayerful, you'll be sinful. (See Matthew 26:41.)

We will study the four areas that every individual must deal with throughout their lives. Even Jesus had to face and pass these tests.

When Satan tempted Christ in the wilderness, each one of the appetites were specifically tested. Three of them are carnal, and one is divine.

We'll begin by defining and explaining the three carnal appetites. We can see them listed together in one verse of Scripture:

> *For all that is in the world — the desires*
> *of the flesh and the desires of the eyes*
> *and pride of life — is not from the Father*
> *but is from the world.*
>
> **1 John 2:16 ESV**

The carnal appetites are the desires of the flesh, the desires of the eyes, and the pride of life. Finally, we'll discuss the fourth—the spiritual appetite, which every believer is responsible for developing themselves.

1. THE DESIRES OF THE FLESH

When you begin to fast and pray, this is the first appetite that fights back against you. The desires of the flesh immediately become apparent. Your body wants to please itself with food.

Remember, anything that your flesh actively resists reveals what your flesh actually wants. For example, though it's good for you, your flesh rejects and resists exercise. Even though we know it's the right choice, we often don't do it because our flesh talks us out of it.

By inspiration of the Holy Spirit, Paul stated that physical exercise was profitable (1 Timothy 4:8). Many are sick and in distress because they've not taken care of their bodies.

As a result, the temple of the Holy Spirit is in chaos and lacks strength because someone was unwilling to take control of their fleshly appetite and desire for comfort. Neglect and irresponsibility can result in many physical problems and sicknesses.

Another example is sleep. Our flesh loves to sleep. No one's flesh (unless it's been trained) wants to wake up and diligently work toward their goals.

God saw this as such a problem that he gave his people warnings about the dangers of laziness. People who love to sleep in and refuse to discipline their flesh to work diligently will suffer lack.

> *How long will you lie there, O sluggard?*
> *When will you arise from your sleep? A*
> *little sleep, a little slumber, a little fold-*
> *ing of the hands to rest, and poverty will*
> *come upon you like a robber, and want*
> *like an armed man.*
>
> *Proverbs 6:9-11 ESV*

Allowing your flesh to have what it wants is a perilous habit and will always lead to destruction. This is because the desires of your flesh are sinful and displeasing to God. When Paul wrote to the Galatians, he listed the works of the flesh:

> *Now the works of the flesh are evident:*
> *sexual immorality, impurity, sensual-*
> *ity, idolatry, sorcery, enmity, strife, jeal-*
> *ousy, fits of anger, rivalries, dissensions,*
> *divisions, envy, drunkenness, orgies, and*
> *things like these.*
>
> *Galatians 5:20-21 ESV*

If your fleshly nature is allowed to control your life, it will produce these kinds of results. Notice that Paul wasn't writing to sinners, but Christians. If Christians let their appetites go unchecked, they will enter into the works of the flesh. That's why Paul encouraged them to walk by the Spirit so they wouldn't gratify the desires of the flesh (Galatians 5:16).

As you fast and pray, it weakens the flesh and its desires. Fasting and prayer give you victory over the flesh and put it into submission. Paul subdued his flesh daily (1 Corinthians 9:27).

Jesus had to subdue his flesh, as well. In the midst of his final preparation for ministry in the wilderness, the devil came to tempt him. He began by tempting his fleshly desires.

> *And after fasting forty days and forty nights, he was hungry. And the tempter came and said to him, "If you are the Son of God, command these stones to become loaves of bread."*
>
> *Matthew 4:2-3 ESV*

During Christ's fasting and prayer, Satan tried to appeal to Jesus' carnal desire to eat. He wanted to pull Jesus out of his spiritual focus and reinvigorate his flesh.

Jesus knew better and rebuked the enemy. He quoted from the book of Deuteronomy. "Man shall not live by bread alone," Jesus said, "but by every word that comes from the mouth of God."

Have you ever considered that what Jesus was really saying was that he wasn't seeking *natural bread*, but *spiritual bread*?

The Word of God is bread for your spirit. How do we know? Jesus is the Word made flesh (John 1:14). However, he also revealed that he was "the bread that came down from heaven" (John 6:41).

The Word of God is spiritual bread from Heaven. When you eat natural food, your flesh becomes stronger. However, when you fast, pray, and read God's Word, your spirit becomes stronger.

It's no surprise that in the most hedonistic societies, like ancient Greece and Rome, feasting and sexual immorality went hand in hand. The flesh wants what pleases it, but it must be controlled and subdued.

2. THE DESIRES OF THE EYES

The second appetite that can become dangerous if left unchecked is the desire of your eyes. What you see and how you see it is imperative.

The book of Proverbs gives instruction regarding

your heart and your life. You have to actively guard yourself against any external influence that would affect your life negatively.

Watch over your heart with all diligence,
For from it flow the springs of life.
Proverbs 4:23 NASB

Although we have five senses, the two that primarily fuel our hearts with information are what we see and hear. If we're going to guard our hearts, we not only have to guard what we see and what we hear, we have to guard how we *process* what we see and hear.

Fear doesn't come by what we see or hear; it comes by how we process what we see or hear.

For example, when Jesus called Peter out onto the stormy sea, Peter did the impossible and walked on water in the midst of the storm.

Notice, the storm didn't change; Peter's *focus* changed. He saw the storm before he stepped out of the boat. When his focus changed, he began to process what he saw differently. It was a transition from faith to fear.

Now, instead of doing the impossible, he began to sink. The only thing that changed was how he processed what his eyes could see. That's the exact problem every believer must deal with when guarding their heart.

In the same way that fear can enter your heart by un-guarded vision, covetousness can enter also. Paul listed jealousy as a carnal work of the flesh.

The desire for things you see can be so dangerous that it can rule your life. Jesus taught:

> *No one can serve two masters, for either he will hate the one and love the other, or he will be devoted to the one and de-spise the other. You cannot serve God and money.*
>
> *Matthew 6:24 ESV*

Many people are controlled by an unholy desire for things. It's not that having things is wrong, but things cannot have you.

Incidentally, that's why tithing and giving are tests that continually measure the state of your heart toward God. It reveals whether you serve God or money.

Consider the story of the rich young ruler who approached Jesus and wanted to become a disciple. After telling Jesus he had followed God's commands since he was a child, Jesus told him that he lacked one thing—giving.

I believe Jesus saw something about this man from which we can learn a vital lesson:

> *Jesus said to him, "If you would be per-*
> *fect, go, sell what you possess and give*
> *to the poor, and you will have treasure*
> *in heaven; and come, follow me."*
> *Matthew 19:21 ESV*

Did Jesus tell anyone else to sell all of their possessions? No. Only this man. Why? Because he must have
discerned that the young ruler had a problem with
possessions ruling his life. The proof is in the man's response to Jesus' command.

> *When the young man heard this he went*
> *away sorrowful, for he had great posses-*
> *sions.*
> *Matthew 19:22 ESV*

He went away sorrowful because he *couldn't* obey Jesus' command. His possessions had control of his life.
It's not that money or possessions are evil; it's the *love* of
money that's the source of all kinds of evil. (See 1 Timothy 6:10.)

That's why the devil worked so hard to entangle Jesus in the desires of the eyes. He wanted Jesus to fall
into the trap of covetousness and the love of money and
possessions. We see it clearly in the wilderness.

*Again, the devil took him to a very high
mountain and showed him all the king-
doms of the world and their glory. And
he said to him, "All these I will give you,
if you will fall down and worship me."*
Matthew 4:8-9 ESV

Satan, who had the authority as the "god of this
world" to give Jesus these things (2 Corinthians 4:4),
was attempting to fill Jesus' eyes and heart with a lust
for possessions.

Jesus actively guarded his heart by using God's Word
to rebuke Satan's temptation. If Satan could have filled
Christ's heart with a love of money and possessions, every evil work would have stemmed from that one sin.

*For the love of money is a root of all
kinds of evils . . .*
1 Timothy 6:10 ESV

Fasting is a form of humbling yourself. It puts life in
perspective. Through fasting and prayer, we realize that
God is all we need.

He is called El Shaddai, which means the "all-suffi-
cient One." He is everything we need and has given us
all we need to live for him (2 Peter 1:3).

Notice the carnal reaction to not having the things for which your eyes have lusted.

> *You desire and do not have, so you mur-*
> *der. You covet and cannot obtain, so you*
> *fight and quarrel. You do not have, be-*
> *cause you do not ask. You ask and do*
> *not receive, because you ask wrongly, to*
> *spend it on your passions.*
>
> *James 4:2-3 ESV*

The appetite of the eyes must be defeated. It's a "self over God" mentality which becomes a form of idolatry. We can have nothing in our lives that takes priority over God—even ourselves. He is always first.

> *But seek first the kingdom of God and*
> *his righteousness, and all these things*
> *will be added to you.*
>
> *Matthew 6:33 ESV*

As his servant, my personal life with God comes before everything. It takes priority over my ministry, my wife, my children, and my possessions. If you put God first, he will put you first.

3. THE PRIDE OF LIFE

The final carnal desire that must be conquered is the pride of life. You could make a strong argument that this should be the first appetite that should be addressed as it's the most dangerous.

The Holy Spirit inspired King Solomon and gave us a warning about the infinite dangers of arrogance.

> *Pride goes before destruction, and a haughty spirit before a fall.*
>
> *Proverbs 16:18 ESV*

Pride was the very thing that caused Lucifer to be ejected from Heaven. Lucifer made his arrogant intentions known with five "I will" statements, which were answered by a resounding, "You won't" from God.

Satan was so deceived by pride that he actually believed he could seat himself on God's throne and be like the Most High. God put a quick end to Lucifer's nonsense and ejected him. Jesus looked back through the tunnel of time and said:

> *I saw Satan fall like lightning from heaven.*
>
> *Luke 10:18 ESV*

There was no second chance for Lucifer. He was promptly cut off from God's presence. God will not share his glory with anyone. It belongs to him alone. (See Isaiah 42:8.)

In the New Testament, we can see the dangers of taking God's glory for ourselves. This is the purest form of pride. Look what happened to King Herod after he gave a speech to the people.

> *And the people were shouting, "The voice of a god, and not of a man!" Immediately an angel of the Lord struck him down, because he did not give God the glory, and he was eaten by worms and breathed his last.*
>
> *Acts 12:22-23 ESV*

All too often, we don't regard pride as a dangerous poison. It's easy to think that because pride is common, it's okay — quite the opposite. Pride is an element that attracts the opposition of God.

> *Clothe yourselves, all of you, with humility toward one another, for "God opposes the proud but gives grace to the humble."*
>
> *1 Peter 5:5 ESV*

Do you see how serious that is? God *opposes* the proud. Do you want God as an opponent? I think not. Especially when you understand what the Apostle Paul wrote to the church in Rome:

> *What then shall we say to these things?*
> *If God is for us, who can be against us?*
> Romans 8:31 ESV

As we see throughout the entire Bible, if God is on your side, no one can defeat you. However, if God is your enemy, your fate is sealed.

I'm sure you can see why the devil so badly wants to pull you into pride. He would love to make God your enemy and ultimately destroy you.

Satan worked hard to pull Jesus into a place of pride during the famous wilderness temptation. He knew that if he could get Christ to fall into pride, destruction would be the result.

I want you to see how slimy and devious this temptation was. Satan appealed to Jesus' heavenly position and calling. Something that seemed to be right on the surface was horribly wrong.

Remember, it's possible to do the right thing for the wrong reasons. This is why Jesus rebuked the Pharisees for their fasting, prayer, and giving practices. Obviously,

God wants us to fast, pray, and give, but the Pharisees were only doing it to be seen by others. In their pride, they wanted to be seen as the most pious men alive.

Jesus called them "whitewashed tombs." He was indicating that although they looked holy on the outside, they were dead and unclean inside. That's what pride does to you.

Look at the exchange that takes place when Satan used pride to tempt Jesus.

> *Then the devil took him to the holy city and set him on the pinnacle of the temple and said to him, "If you are the Son of God, throw yourself down, for it is written, 'He will command his angels concerning you,' and 'On their hands they will bear you up, lest you strike your foot against a stone.'"*
>
> *Matthew 4:5-6 ESV*

Satan was trying to quote Scripture to Jesus to get him to fall. How foolish is Satan? He tried to use the Word of God against the Word of God.

Was Jesus saying that Psalm 91, the passage Satan quoted, wasn't true? Of course not. He refused to let Satan use it out of context to cause him to stumble.

Think of the magnitude of this temptation. What if Satan could have tricked Christ into committing suicide rather than completing the act of redemption on the cross? What a foolish and devastating ending that would have been.

Imagine how many people have been destroyed by pride before they could accomplish their purpose. Pride, the most deadly of all the attacks of the devil, must be avoided at all costs.

Fight hard against pride. I think it's interesting that throughout Scripture, fasting was a method used by God's people to humble themselves. It serves that same purpose today.

This is why fasting and prayer need to be a regular part of your life. As long as we have a carnal nature, pride will be a temptation. As I wrote when I began this chapter, self-control will keep your carnal nature from taking over.

I don't believe that it was an accident that as soon as Jesus was filled with the Holy Spirit, the Spirit led him into the wilderness to fast and pray. Would Jesus have been able to withstand these temptations had he not been fasting and praying? I don't believe this sequence of events was random.

The Spirit of God knows what you need before you need it. That's why it's so vital to rely on the leading of the Holy Spirit (Romans 8:14). If you will dedicate your-self to fasting, prayer, and the Word of God, failure and defeat will never be your story. You can be constantly victorious. As Solomon wrote, the path of the righteous shines "brighter and brighter" (Proverbs 4:18).

4. THE DESIRES OF THE SPIRIT

Finally, the fourth desire is that of the spirit. The desires of your human spirit are unified with those of the Holy Spirit because you have been made new in Christ.

The wonderful thing about spiritual desires is that they lead to the supernatural blessing of the Lord.

John G. Lake, a man of God who saw hundreds of thousands of miracles in his ministry, said that if he could impart one quality to the body of Christ, it would be spiritual hunger.[2] Of course, the reason for this can be clearly seen in Jesus' Sermon on the Mount.

Blessed are those who hunger and thirst
for righteousness, For they shall be filled.
Matthew 5:6 NKJV

Did you notice that filling is based upon hunger? Not everyone is being filled, only those who are hungry and thirsty.

Hunger and thirst will make you do things you normally wouldn't do. They're driving forces, catalysts of action.

I had just finished preaching a Sunday morning church service in one of our extended meetings. Afterward, as we usually do, we planned to go eat lunch with the pastor and his family.

I typically don't eat breakfast on Sunday morning before I preach, and as a result, I was famished. As I drove down the road, my stomach sounded like it was inhabited by an angry creature that was yelling at me.

Suddenly, a very familiar smell blew through the vents in my car — french fries. I looked up and saw what at that moment may as well have been the Promised Land. It was the golden arches of McDonald's.

(I can hear you judging me as I write.)

In milliseconds, I experienced a multiplicity of thoughts and made a few mental calculations.

I thought about the fact that after I finally got to the restaurant, it would probably be at least another twenty minutes before any food would come from the kitchen.

My stomach growled louder. The french fry smell called to me like a newspaper boy on the street shouting the headlines. *French fries! Burgers!*

In the final moments, before my car passed the driveway and my opportunity for instant gratification was lost, I swung my steering wheel with the accuracy of a NASCAR driver. Horns blared as I cut other drivers off, and I glided smoothly into the drive-thru.

I continued the trip to the restaurant while finishing two cheeseburgers, fries, a four-piece nugget, (and a diet Coke to keep it healthy).

Obviously, I don't recommend doing this. You shouldn't eat two lunches in a row. (Didn't we start this chapter with self-control? How did we end up here?)

The point is, hunger is a strong, driving force. Your hunger will provoke you to action.

That's why Jesus taught that those who are hungry for righteousness will be filled. Why? Because their hunger for righteousness will provoke them to take actions of righteousness. That leads to being filled.

EATING MAKES YOU HUNGRIER

One of the paradoxes of the kingdom is that unlike natural eating, when you eat spiritually, it makes you even hungrier. The Psalmist understood the fulfillment that comes from the Lord and wrote:

> *How sweet are your words to my taste,*
> *sweeter than honey to my mouth!*
> *Psalm 119:103 ESV*

When you see the effects it has in your life, your spiritual appetite grows in strength. Jeremiah knew the benefits of seeking after God and staying hungry.

> *Your words were found, and I ate them,*
> *And Your word was to me the joy and*
> *rejoicing of my heart . . .*
> *Jeremiah 15:16 ESV*

Spiritual hunger can be defined as "having a strong desire, craving, displaying the need for God."

In his most significant theological work, *Pensées*, Blaise Pascal, famed 17th century French mathematician, physicist, inventor, philosopher, writer, and theologian, wrote, "There is a God-shaped vacuum in the heart of every man which cannot be filled by any created thing, but only by God, the Creator made known through Jesus."[3]

We desperately need the Lord. That's why Christ quoted from Deuteronomy during his temptation.

> *. . . man does not live by bread alone, but*
> *man lives by every word that comes from*
> *the mouth of the LORD.*
> *Deuteronomy 8:3 ESV*

All spiritual success hinges upon this one discipline — walking by the Spirit. God inspired Paul to pen this essential verse of Scripture to the Galatians:

> *But I say, walk by the Spirit, and you*
> *will not gratify the desires of the flesh.*
> *Galatians 5:16 ESV*

Can anyone truly conquer the three carnal appetites and yield to the spiritual appetite without fasting and prayer? Your answer should be a resounding no.

This is why we're commanded to pray without ceasing (1 Thessalonians 5:17), and it thoroughly explains why Christ expected his children to fast (Mark 2:20).

Now you understand why Bishop Oyedepo says, "If you're not prayerful, you'll be sinful." There's only one way to please the Lord — we must continually conquer the three carnal appetites, feed the spiritual appetite, and yield to God's presence.

God isn't pleased with any kind of fasting that doesn't crucify the flesh.

Chapter Nine

THE DANGER OF THE DANIEL FAST

This will probably be the most controversial chapter in any book I've ever written. How dare I come against the body of Christ's beloved Daniel Fast? Before you skip this chapter or blow it off, however, I want you to consider some fascinating biblical facts about this so-called Daniel Fast.

As we seek to please God with our actions and follow his instructions, it's important to understand what the Lord wants his children to do.

If the Daniel Fast is biblical, then, by all means, let us continue to engage in it. On the other hand, if it's not, let's toss it to the side and seek the Lord in a scriptural way. Above any tradition or trend, we want to obey the Word of God in every circumstance.

WHAT IS THE DANIEL FAST?

Before we accept or reject the Daniel Fast, it's essential to understand what it is as defined in Scripture. As you might guess, it's described in the Old Testament book of Daniel.

In 605 BC, Nebuchadnezzar II became the king of the Chaldean Empire. Eight years later, he invaded Jerusalem and took control. Daniel, Shadrach, Meshach, Abednego, and other fellow captives were taken to the Chaldean capital of Babylon to study literature.

All of the young men who were brought to the capital were offered the royal food and wine during the three years of their training. Daniel, however, refused and only ate what was pleasing to God.

The king's meat may have been defiled in the sight of the Jews (possibly not completely drained of blood or previously offered to idols). This meat would have been forbidden for God's people.

Daniel chose a diet of vegetables and water. Though the guard charged with their training was concerned for their health while eating such a diet, he permitted them to test it for ten days.

At the end of the allotted time, the guard was impressed with Daniel and his friends' appearance and physical and mental health compared to the other young men and allowed them to continue on this diet for the next three years. When the king inspected them at the end of that period, they were ten times better than all the magicians and enchanters in his kingdom. (See Daniel 1:5-20.)

God blessed them for their devotion to his laws and commandments. God gave them favor in the kingdom, and others became very jealous of it.

Fifty-eight years later, Cyrus the Great, king of Persia, captured Babylon. In the third year of his reign, Daniel received a vision and a word and began to mourn, fast, and pray. (See Daniel 10:1-3.)

During those twenty-one days, he consumed no meat, wine, or "tasty foods." The last phrase may be a bit vague. Different translations render the Hebrew differently. The King James says, "pleasant bread," while the more liberal New Living Translation uses the term "rich food." A footnote in the New American Standard says that the phrase could be translated in the most literal form, "bread of desirability."

Daniel chapters 1 and 10 are the passages most-commonly used to define the Daniel Fast. In modern-day practice, those who participate in this fast limit their food choices to whole grains, fruits, vegetables, beans, nuts, and seeds. Typically, no animal products are consumed.

Also excluded are processed foods, additives, preservatives, flavorings, sweeteners, caffeine, alcohol, oils, and products made with white flours. (Obviously, many of these options weren't even available in Daniel's day.)

The Daniel Fast typically takes place over twenty-one days, the same amount of time Daniel was engaged in "fasting" and prayer. However, this leads us to another critical question . . .

DID DANIEL PLAN TO FAST FOR 21 DAYS?

Daniel was praying and expecting an answer from the Lord. *He did not know how long it would take to receive that answer.* That's a significant point! Let me explain.

This wasn't the first time Daniel fasted. In Daniel chapter 9, after reading Jeremiah's prophecies, Daniel began to fast and pray for his people.

> *Then I turned my face to the Lord God, seeking him by prayer and pleas for mercy with fasting and sackcloth and ashes.*
> *Daniel 9:3 ESV*

Notice that this passage says nothing about the types of food that Daniel ate during this fast. That's because he didn't eat; he fasted. As a Jew, Daniel would have been very familiar with fasting, what it meant, and how it was done. As we've previously covered, the Hebrew word for *fast* means to close or cover the mouth.

Daniel ate nothing during this fast *because he was fasting.* Does the Bible say that Daniel fasted in chapter 1 or chapter 10? No.

Daniel chapter 1 refers to what he's doing as a *diet.* He couldn't have sustained his life during the three years of training by only drinking water.

In the same way, Daniel was prepared to wait for his answer indefinitely. He didn't know when the Lord would answer his prayer. The Holy Spirit, who inspired all Scripture, didn't see fit to call the dietary restriction in chapter 10 a fast.

What Daniel did in chapter 10 is similar to what he did in chapter 1. It was a special diet that honored God as he spent time in mourning, but he continued to eat and did not fast. His answer did not come until the twenty-fourth day (Daniel 10:4).

Though I'm sure Daniel spent a very sobering twenty-one days in mourning and prayer, that doesn't seem to be the common trend with the modern-day "Daniel Fast."

Many Christians seem to be more enamored with the available options or guidelines of the fast itself than seeking the Lord in prayer.

WRONG FOCUS = FLIPPANT FASTING

One thing that grieves me is seeing Christians take fasting and prayer so lightly. While I'm happy to see many Christians moving back toward dedication to the Lord in some way, I'm also concerned about how we define dedication.

Every January, as people prepare for their Daniel Fast, I see social media blowing up with all of the recipes and ingredients that people will use to cook the big meals they'll be eating during the Daniel Fast. They've got an entire menu!

A simple Google search for "Daniel Fast recipes" will yield results like Quinoa Chili, Chickpea Curry over a bed of rice, Mexican sweet potatoes with black bean salsa, and creamy cilantro sauce, or roasted vegetables over wild rice and a huge dollop of hummus and sour cashew cream.

Need dessert? Grab yourself some Daniel Fast banana bread or Daniel Fast cobbler! It's ridiculous.

People spend more time planning their meals for this fast than they do when they're eating normally. Christians become so proud of their Daniel Fast dishes that they have to capture perfect Instagram and Facebook images of each meal.

Are we focused on humbling ourselves before the

Lord in prayer? No. We've created some weird subculture of the "Daniel Fast Culinary Club." If we think it's pleasing to God, we're only fooling ourselves.

You may think I'm too harsh, but let me ask you a question that is paramount as we desire to seek the Lord in fasting and prayer.

IS THE FLESH BEING CRUCIFIED?

One of the main functions of fasting is to weaken the flesh. Why? Because as Paul taught, it's the source of wickedness.

> *For I know that nothing good dwells in me, that is, in my flesh. For I have the desire to do what is right, but not the ability to carry it out.*
>
> *Romans 7:18 ESV*

Furthermore, Paul taught the Galatians that the flesh is always at war with the spirit and attempting to keep it from doing what it should (Galatians 5:17).

Christ was very clear about this principle when admonishing his disciples to dedicate themselves to lives of prayer. "The spirit indeed is willing," he told them, "But the flesh is weak." (See Matthew 26:41.)

You must win the war between your flesh and spirit to please God with your actions. Notice the way Paul handled this thought when dealing with the church in Galatia:

> *But I say, walk by the Spirit, and you will not gratify the desires of the flesh. For the desires of the flesh are against the Spirit, and the desires of the Spirit are against the flesh, for these are opposed to each other, to keep you from doing the things you want to do.*
>
> *Galatians 5:16-17 ESV*

Is this sort of "Daniel Fasting" crucifying or weakening your flesh? Absolutely not. Do you realize you could faithfully adhere to this modern-day Daniel Fast and gain weight?

The flesh is still being given all the strength it needs to continue ruling your life. It doesn't resemble what Daniel did during his time of mourning.

More importantly, neither the Jews nor New Testament believers practiced anything like the modern Daniel Fast and dared to call it fasting. Let's call it what it truly is: *eating*.

THE DANIEL FAST WAS NEVER REPLICATED

It has always been amusing to me that most Christians choose the Daniel Fast when deciding to fast. Even though, as previously mentioned, the Bible doesn't call it a fast, nor is it found anywhere else in Scripture.

As you read through the Old Testament, you'll find many places where God's people fasted. When they did, they fasted totally.

In some instances, they didn't even drink water (Esther 4:16). Other times, even the livestock were forced to fast with the population (Jonah 3:7).

The same is true in the New Testament. Neither the Jews, Jesus, John's disciples, or any Apostles ate anything during times of fasting and prayer. To fast is to refrain from eating.

With all of the biblical examples of fasting and prayer we have, why do so many Christians choose the "Daniel Fast?" Because it's the easiest on the flesh.

It should be significant to every believer that every time a true fast was observed in Scripture, they ate nothing. This is God's pattern of the fasting that should accompany prayer.

The Daniel Fast is not a fast at all; it's merely a diet that Daniel used for what may have been an indefinite period of time while he waited on the Lord.

ISN'T IT A GOOD STARTING POINT FOR BEGINNERS?

Some may argue that the Daniel Fast is a good place to start for believers who are new to fasting. Maybe it's a great way to help them get their feet wet.

I disagree. Would you argue that someone who is newly saved should only live a holy life 65% of the time? After all, we're letting them ease into Christianity, right? I'm sure you're as appalled at that idea as I am.

If God has commanded his children to do something, we must do it. We don't negotiate the commands or expectations of God. We obey.

Similarly, why would we encourage beginners to engage in a fast that isn't truly a fast? They might as well continue eating normally. It will do them just as much good.

In my opinion, the best way for beginners to get involved is to engage in fasting for a shorter time. They might start by fasting from sunrise to sunset. (See Judges 20:26.)

As they continue to press into God's presence, they may want to fast for three days (Esther 4:16) or seven days (1 Samuel 31:13).

It's important to remember that while Jesus does expect us to fast throughout our lives, believers are never commanded to fast for any specific length of time.

The best way to fast is to be led by the Spirit of God. Do it by faith and with a humble yet expectant heart. Fasting and prayer are actions of faith and are promised to be rewarded by God, who is continually monitoring our private dedication (See Matthew 6:6,18.)

DID DANIEL EVEN DO THE DANIEL FAST?

I want to finish this chapter with a fascinating thought. Did Daniel engage in what we call the Daniel Fast?

When we read Daniel 10:3, we assume that he only removed meat, wine, and pleasant bread (or rich foods) from his diet. But what if he didn't? What if it was more than that? It's possible.

Finis Jennings Dake was a Pentecostal minister and author. In 1963, he produced the Dake Annotated Reference Bible, which contains 35,000 notes on Scripture. Dake could quote the entire Bible verbatim — a gift that was tested publicly on live radio.

His commentary (though considered by some to be personal and not biblical) is expansive and insightful because of his unique gift. It's considered by many to be one of the most revelatory reference Bibles in existence.

In his commentary on Daniel 10:3, Dake alludes to the fact that this passage may be describing a full fast and not a diet as many today have interpreted this verse.

> **[no pleasant bread, neither came flesh nor wine
> in my mouth]** This is the same as saying that he
> was on a total fast, not on a diet as some today
> call a Daniel's fast.[1]

Interestingly, it may be possible that Daniel didn't eat anything at all during these three weeks of mourning. He was genuinely fasting if he didn't (though the Bible doesn't specifically say so). If not, it was a diet, much like what took place in chapter 1.

The critical thing to remember is that fasting, as modeled throughout the Scriptures, is a practice of totally abstaining from food to weaken the flesh and seek the face of God in prayer.

Our desire should be to follow the biblical model of Christ and the Apostles, press in through prayer, and humbly, yet boldly, believe God for miracles.

Chapter Ten
WHAT WILL FASTING DO TO MY BODY?

One of the wonderful things about the God we serve is that his wisdom is infinite (Psalm 147:5). Isaiah understood the staggering depths of God's wisdom and understanding when he wrote:

> *Have you not known? Have you not heard? The LORD is the everlasting God, the Creator of the ends of the earth. He does not faint or grow weary; his understanding is unsearchable.*
>
> *Isaiah 40:28 ESV*

Although when God created and prescribed fasting it had spiritual meaning and significance, he also knew it would give his people practical health benefits. As the creator of our bodies, he understands what they need to function properly and remain strong.

A PATTERN OF REST

I find it very interesting that, throughout Scripture, God modeled a pattern of rest. In the beginning, he created the earth and everything in it in six days and rested on the seventh day.

But God didn't only rest from working on the seventh day. He highlighted that day for a purpose. He blessed it and made it holy.

> *So God blessed the seventh day and made it holy, because on it God rested from all his work that he had done in creation.*
> *Genesis 2:3 ESV*

Similarly, as the Jews traveled through the wilderness, God only provided manna for six days each week. On the seventh day, no manna was available.

Though they gathered extra manna to eat on the seventh day ahead of time, could this day with no food have been a pattern that God was showing his people?

Did you know that this principle of rest extended to

their land, as well? God made sure that even their farms had time to recover from the previous six years of work. Look at God's command:

> *But in the seventh year there shall be a Sabbath of solemn rest for the land, a Sabbath to the LORD. You shall not sow your field or prune your vineyard.*
> *Leviticus 25:4 ESV*

God cares about his creation. He cares about his people most of all. Though Christ encouraged hard work for the kingdom, when his disciples had completed their tasks, he ensured that they rested themselves properly.

The Lord showed me a passage of Scripture one year when I had been running extra hard. I had almost taken pride in how hard I'd been working for the Lord — so hard that I almost burnt out.

Burnout — total exhaustion — is not God's desire for his workers. Remember this: God cares about you *more* than the work you can do for him.

Amid my exhaustion, as I was praying for more strength, the Lord spoke a very simple word to me that splashed over my spirit like ice-cold water in the morning. He said, "You're not my only worker."

That blew my mind. Of course, I knew I wasn't his

only worker, but I thought he'd be pleased with me for running as hard as I could.

I began to realize that God would rather have us work effectively for an extended time rather than a few years of nonstop work until we've collapsed from exhaustion. He led me to this passage:

> *The apostles returned to Jesus and told him all that they had done and taught. And he said to them, "Come away by yourselves to a desolate place and rest a while." For many were coming and going, and they had no leisure even to eat.*
>
> *Mark 6:30-31 ESV*

Do you see that rather than telling them to get back to work, Jesus put a premium on their rest? It's a principle that God has instituted from the beginning.

In the same way, our bodies need to rest from food and digestion. You may not realize it, but many toxins are stored in your body from years of eating.

One of the many benefits of fasting is that it gives your digestive system a rest and expels toxins that have been building up inside your body.

In his eye-opening book, *Toxic Relief*, Dr. Don Colbert writes, "Fasting is a powerful, natural way to cleanse your body from the burden of excess toxins, such as toxic fats, and from many other chemicals and toxins that cause degenerative diseases. Fasting is the safest and best way to heal the body from degenerative diseases caused by being overfed with the wrong nutrition.[1]

It's staggering how many benefits are contained in the simple principle of rest from digestion through fasting. As we've covered in another chapter, the Pharisees and the disciples fasted for two, nonconsecutive, twenty-four-hour periods every week.

In the following sections, I'll provide a summary of the positive results fasting has on your body. I'll also discuss the effects and feelings you can expect to experience while on short and extended fasts, so you're not taken by surprise.

Finally, we'll discuss some of the main reasons people refuse to fast or break their fasts before they planned to do so. You can stay strong and seek the Lord!

FASTING AND OBESITY

The more I learn, the more things surprise me. I'm the kind of person that thrives on finding solutions. When I figure something out that I previously didn't know, it's like finding a key that unlocks multiple doors to move forward with life. It's somewhat like solving a mystery.

Recently, I heard Dr. Rhonda Patrick, a long life specialist, being interviewed by well-known podcast host and TV personality, Joe Rogan.

She made a comment on his show that was so stunning, I had to stop the video, rewind, and listen again to make sure I heard it correctly.

She stated that over fifty percent of people in hospitals are being treated for Metabolic Syndrome, which is made up of type two diabetes, high blood pressure, excess body fat, high triglyceride levels, and low levels of "good" HDL cholesterol.[2]

This means that half of the patients could have easily prevented (and could cure) their issues by eating a disciplined diet and exercising regularly.

In fact, according to recent studies, over one-third of Americans are now dealing with Metabolic Syndrome.[3]

Obesity is one of the leading causes of health problems in our world today. It leads to so many deadly sicknesses and disorders.

At the time of writing, over forty percent of Americans are considered overweight or obese, according to U.S. News & World Report.[4]

The medical literature seems to be clear; the most effective way of staying healthy and living a long life is to make wise eating choices and exercise three to five times each week.

That doesn't sound revelatory, does it? Sounds like self-control. Sounds like self-discipline.

Regular fasting is one of the easiest ways to keep your body in check. Not only does it give your digestive system a rest, but it also keeps your carnal nature from taking over and overeating, which will eventually harm the temple of the Holy Spirit.

We cannot beat around the bush. Obesity is dangerous and displeasing to God. I'm not writing this to condemn you if you're obese; I want you to understand that God wants you to be healthy and live a long, productive life in his kingdom.

When I was growing up, I heard many messages on being free from drugs, alcohol, nicotine, tobacco, and pornography, but there was rarely any teaching on overeating and gluttony.

Do you realize that obesity kills more people every year than cancer, liver disease, and overdoses combined?[5] It's far deadlier, yet we don't view it in the same way.

We should. We have a responsibility to honor God with our bodies as they are his property.

> *. . . You do not belong to yourself, for God bought you with a high price. So you must honor God with your body.*
> *1 Corinthians 6:19-20 NLT*

Whether you're fasting for an extended period, a short time, or intermittently each day, fasting will benefit you as you win the war against obesity.

While weight loss is not the goal of biblical, Christian fasting, it's a side effect that God knew would benefit his children as they continued to seek him in fasting and prayer. If correctly done, even the sunrise to sunset fast would help your body and give you health benefits.

FASTING, YOUR LIVER, AND KIDNEYS

It's important to remember that your liver, kidneys, urinary tract, colon, lungs, and skin are your body's primary elimination channels. As Dr. Colbert writes, "Fasting allows your liver to catch up on its internal cleansing and detoxification."[6]

When you fast, it's essential to drink plenty of water, which protects your kidneys and helps you avoid kidney stones. The Institute of Medicine recommends that men drink about 3 liters of water each day, while women should drink approximately 2.2 liters.[7]

FASTING AND YOUR CHOLESTEROL

According to the Mayo Clinic, "Regular fasting can decrease your low-density lipoprotein (LDL), or 'bad,' cholesterol. It's also thought that fasting can improve the way your body metabolizes sugar. This can reduce your risk of gaining weight and developing diabetes, which are both risk factors for heart disease."[8]

If you're unaware, high cholesterol can be the cause of gallstones, memory loss, strokes, the formation of plaques that lead to Alzheimer's disease, high blood pressure, and, as previously mentioned, heart disease.[9]

FASTING AND YOUR INSULIN

Sadly, type 2 diabetes has become extremely prevalent in the United States and around the world. The Center for Disease Control has reported that one in three American adults is diabetic or prediabetic.[10]

Either the pancreas has suffered so much abuse that it will no longer produce necessary amounts of insulin, or the blood cells have become "insulin resistant." If left unchecked, it can be deadly.

Dr. Jason Fung, author of *The Complete Guide to Fasting*, studied the effects of fasting among men with type 2 diabetes for ten months.

"The thing that surprised me most was how quickly patients got better," Dr. Fung said. "Even after 25 years of diabetes, the maximum time it took to get off insulin was eighteen days. All three patients improved their diabetes to the point that they no longer required insulin, and it only took from five to eighteen days in this study."[11]

When you see how type 2 diabetes develops, it only makes sense that even intermittent fasting would produce these positive changes in your body.

FASTING AND YOUR BLOOD PRESSURE

As previously covered, fasting can lower your cholesterol, which, in turn, reduces plaque and the hardening of your arteries. In the absence of plaque build up in your arteries, blood can flow freely.

As a result, your heart doesn't have to work as hard, and your blood pressure, following suit, will go down.

Even the Fresh Prince of Bel-Air, movie star Will Smith, claimed he no longer needed his blood pressure medication after only ten days of fasting.[12]

FASTING AND YOUR STEM CELLS

Stem cells are your body's raw material from which all other cells with special functions are made, including blood cells, liver cells, nerve cells, and cardiac cells. Stem cells are the only cells in the body that have the ability to generate other cell types.

They're very valuable and have sparked recent interest in the scientific and medical communities. They can help us understand how diseases occur, be guided into replacing diseased cells, as well as allow doctors and pharmaceutical companies to test new drugs for safety and quality.[13]

However, as people age, their intestinal stem cells lose the ability to regenerate, making it harder to recover from gastrointestinal infections or other intestinal problems.

A study completed at the Massachusetts Institute of Technology (MIT), one of the world's leading research universities, found that a twenty-four-hour fast can reverse the loss of stem cell function. Fasting drastically improves stem cells' ability to regenerate.

Omer Yilmaz, an assistant professor of biology at MIT, said, "Fasting has many effects in the intestine, which include boosting regeneration as well as potential uses in any type of ailment that impinges on the intestine, such as infections or cancers."[14]

Researchers at USC discovered that prolonged fasting forces the body to use stores of glucose, fat, and ketones, but it also breaks down a significant portion of white blood cells.

During each fasting cycle, this depletion of white blood cells induces changes that trigger stem cell-based regeneration of new immune system cells. They found that fasting may slow aging, tumor progression, and risk of cancer.[15]

These are massive breakthroughs in research, and I'm very interested to see further development as more studies are completed. It's so faith-building to see how God created our bodies to heal itself as we faithfully obey his Word.

FASTING AND SUGAR ADDICTION

Although this may seem like a trivial section to some, sugar addiction—becoming a "carboholic"—may be the leading cause of sickness and death in America.

I've already shown you that obesity and its effects kill more people than anything else, but did you know that sugar addiction is the root cause of obesity?

As the American Diabetes Association has reported, sugar can activate the "pleasure center circuitry" of the brain in much the same way that drugs or alcohol do.[16]

Research from the University of Bordeaux in France suggests that sugar may be *more* addictive than cocaine.

Forty-three rats were placed in cages with two levers. One delivered an intravenous dose of cocaine, while the other gave them a sip of highly sweetened water.

At the end of the fifteen-day trial, forty of the forty-three rats consistently opted for the sugar water over the cocaine.

To further test this hypothesis, they introduced twenty-four more rats to this test. However, these rats were already addicted to cocaine. At the end of ten days, the majority of them preferred the sugar water.[17]

Using fMRI to scan brain activity, neuroscientists have demonstrated that sugar leads to dopamine release in the nucleus accumbens. This is an area of the brain associated with motivation, novelty, and reward. It's the same brain region implicated in response to cocaine and heroin.[18]

Sugar has become an addiction. In the same way the Lord is displeased when his children are controlled by drugs or alcohol, he is also displeased when they are controlled by sugar.

Not only does it destroy the temple of the Holy Spirit, it becomes an idol to you. When I was in Bible school, Brother Kenneth E. Hagin told us a story about his life.

When he was a much younger man, he began working in construction. Every day when he would walk home, he would pass a shop that sold ice-cold Coca-Cola.

Now and then, he would stop in and get a Coke. His visits grew more frequent until he was going in for a Coke every single day. He told us that it got to the point where he couldn't even walk past that shop without going inside to get one.

Brother Hagin became convicted. The Lord told him that Coca Cola was ruling his life. In his mid-eighties he testified to us that after the Lord spoke to him, he never drank another Coke for the rest of his life. Look what Paul wrote:

> *"All things are lawful for me," but not all things are helpful. "All things are lawful for me," but I will not be dominated by anything.*
>
> *1 Corinthians 6:12 ESV*

The Apostle Paul understood this principle. Is it wrong to drink a Coke? No. But it's definitely wrong to be dominated by any substance, including Coca-Cola.

Fasting will help you break your sugar addiction. When you fast, try not to fill yourself with sugary liquids. Don't fast food only to drink 800-calorie lattes from your favorite coffee shop or gallons of juice.

It's okay to have juice and coffee while you're fasting; just don't go overboard.

Drink plenty of water and take care of your body. The Lord will use your times of fasting to touch you spiritually *and* physically.

HOW WILL I FEEL WHEN FASTING?

First, let me state the obvious. You will be hungry. You may laugh reading that, but I've had people tell me that they can't fast because they get too hungry. There will be a period of hunger.

You're not somehow unspiritual or lack faith because you feel hungry. When Jesus finished fasting, he was hungry, too (Matthew 4:2).

If you fast properly, however, your hunger should subside as you enter extended fasting. Don't get nervous. A healthy body can go without food for an extended period of time before it becomes detrimental. As we just covered, it has positive—not negative—effects.

In his classic book on fasting, *God's Chosen Fast*, Arthur Wallis lists the three stages of fasting that believers will experience:

> We may usually distinguish three phases through which the body passes during a long fast (though they are not always clearly defined but tend to overlap, and the duration of each varies greatly with the individual).
>
> The first phase is marked by a craving for food, which may last for a couple of days or longer. Once this passes, though there may continue to

be a pleasurable sensation at the thought of food, there is no craving or strong temptation.

The second phase is marked by a feeling of weakness and faintness, which may last for two or three days or even much longer. At this point every movement of the body seems to require an effort of the will. In many respects this is the most difficult part of the fast, and some may find it necessary to rest a good deal. The gradual disappearance of this sense of weakness is a signal that the body has eliminated its grosser wastes and poisons.

The third and easiest is the phase of growing strength, with little or no concern about food and only occasional and decreasing spasms of weakness. At this stage the person fasting often feels that he or she could continue the fast indefinitely without any great effort.[19]

In my personal experience, after three or four days, the hunger and weakness subside, and I feel energized. However, no matter how you feel, remember that fasting isn't a vacation. It's a time to humble yourself and consecrate your life to the Lord.

Although it holds many benefits, it's not supposed to be "fun." It's a solemn act of dedication that will produce a breakthrough in your life and ministry. I want to encourage you to do it by faith and watch what God will do in and through you.

5 COMMON REASONS FASTING FAILS

I want to give you a few reasons why people may break their fasts early and feel guilty, as I did in the story I shared with you in the chapter on *10 Reasons to Fast and Pray.*

1. Not understanding the power and purpose of fasting. As I shared with you previously, I used to hate fasting. I would often break my fasts before the time I had set aside was completed.

Even though the Bible doesn't prescribe any set length for fasting, if you've set out to give God a specific amount of time in fasting, do what you've vowed.

For example, many people give God twenty-one days of fasting and prayer at the beginning of each year. If you've set aside twenty-one days, be faithful to complete them. Don't allow your flesh or the enemy to stop you from paying your vows to God.

When you understand why we fast and pray as well as the benefits included, it gives you the fuel you need to complete the fasts that you've consecrated to God.

2. Failing to feast on the Word of God. It's essential to understand that God's Word is our spiritual bread. Jesus said that his words are spiritual life (John 6:63).

Christ, who is the Word made flesh, is also the bread that came down from Heaven (John 6:51). The Word is bread. Jesus used this concept to rebuke Satan in the wilderness when he was tempted to break his fast.

> *But he answered, "It is written, 'Man shall not live by bread alone, but by every word that comes from the mouth of God.'"*
> *Matthew 4:4 ESV*

When you're fasting, it's not a time to sleep the fast away or binge-watch your favorite show or movies. It's a time to pray and read God's Word. Dedicate yourself to the Lord by reading his Word daily. If I'm sufficiently feeding my spirit, I've noticed that it curbs my hunger. This is not to say that you won't be hungry while fasting, but failure to fill yourself with Scripture will lead to breaking your fast before you planned.

Part of the reason this happens is that when you haven't read the Bible or spent time praying, the enemy will use that to encourage you to stop fasting.

"Oh, you're not really pressing in," he'll whisper. "You might as well eat something and fast another time." Don't fall for that temptation. Instead, pray or read God's Word right then. Defeat the temptation of the enemy.

3. Not taking time to pray. Prayer is a spiritual action that gives you the strength to carry out what you're called to do—even things you don't want to do.

Jesus didn't want to be crucified, but he surrendered his will to God through the power of prayer. Jesus prayed regarding the cross and his impending crucifixion:

> *"Father, if you are willing, remove this*
> *cup from me. Nevertheless, not my will,*
> *but yours, be done."*
>
> *Luke 22:42 ESV*

Prayer contains a strengthening power that will keep you connected each day you fast. You must dedicate significant time to prayer during fasting.

As Bishop David Oyedepo once said, "If you're not praying at least an hour a day [while fasting], you might as well eat something." Fasting isn't a hunger strike.

Prayer empowers you to overcome temptation in every form—including the temptation to break your fast and eat again. Look how Jesus trained his disciples when they were failing in prayer:

*Watch and pray that you may not en-
ter into temptation. The spirit indeed is
willing, but the flesh is weak."*
                            Matthew 26:41 ESV

Your spirit wants to please God with fasting and
prayer, but your flesh wants to eat. Prayer is the solution
to letting your spirit win this age-old battle.

4. Not separating yourself. I understand that everyone can't lock themselves in a prayer closet for twenty-
one days and skip out on life to pray and fast. However,
when you are fasting, your life should look different
than at other times.

There is a reason that Jesus went into the wilderness
to fast and pray. We must work hard to remove all dis-
tractions from our lives as we seek the Lord.

One of the reasons fasting often fails is because people don't guard themselves against others. There will
always be work dinners, birthday parties, get-togethers,
and many other reasons to break your fast and "start
again tomorrow."

By simply saying no and staying home as much as
possible, you can avoid these temptations and create
your own "wilderness" in which to seek the face of the
Lord.

Don't make the mistake of living life normally when you should be dedicating yourself to a time of prayer and fasting.

5. *Not starting.* Procrastination is one of the deadliest traps that we face. We're not saying "I refuse to fast," we're saying that we'll do it later.

Set goals ahead of time. Are you drinking all liquids? Just water? How long will you fast? What are you praying about during the fast? Set your goals and begin!

> *No discipline is enjoyable while it is happening—it's painful! But afterward there will be a peaceful harvest of right living for those who are trained in this way.*
> *Hebrews 12:11 NLT*

I believe that as you fast and pray, the impossible will become possible for you and that God would lift you up and set you head and shoulders above the rest.

My people are destroyed for lack of knowledge.
—God

Chapter Eleven

FREQUENTLY ASKED QUESTIONS ABOUT FASTING

If you've never fasted before, it might seem like a daunting task to stop eating for an extended time. Some may equate it with starvation and be concerned that it will negatively affect their body.

As I've shown you in a previous chapter, many health benefits accompany fasting. It's something God created to refresh your body.

There are some questions, however, that don't require an entire chapter to answer. They are more easily and quickly answered. This chapter is dedicated to answering some of the most frequently asked questions we get from people who want to fast and pray.

If you have a question that's not answered in this book, please feel free to contact our ministry.

HOW SHOULD I BEGIN MY FAST?

It's wise to prepare your body for what's to come, especially if you're planning to do an extended fast or even a shorter, water-only fast.

If you're going to do the latter, it may be a good idea to begin cutting back on coffee, tea, and sugary drinks as early as a week ahead of time.

This may help curb the caffeine and sugar withdrawals and headaches after you begin fasting. Most people don't realize how addicted their bodies are to caffeine and sugar until they fast.

Dr. Otto Buchinger was a German physician who dedicated himself to studying the therapeutic benefits of fasting and was credited as the first to document the beneficial effects of fasting on a number of diseases.

In his book, *About Fasting*, he recommends that you eat a diet consisting only of fresh fruit on the last day before fasting.

He suggests that the "fruit day" ensures that the last meal left in your bowels is fruit, which causes less decay than other food residues.[2]

On the spiritual side, ask the Lord to strengthen you during your fast. Set goals in prayer, prepare specific requests, and attach the correlating Scriptures to them. Decide on a Bible reading plan, and seek the Lord.

HOW DO I PROPERLY END MY FAST?

When you break your fast, you must use wisdom so that you don't injure yourself. If you've only fasted for a few days, you may return to normal eating without any problem. However, if you've just finished an extended fast — particularly an extended, water-only fast — here are some steps to take as you begin eating again.

First, as a rule of thumb, for every seven days you've fasted, take one day to reacclimate yourself to eating. During this reentry period, eat foods that are easy on your digestive system.

During extended fasting, your stomach shrinks, and your digestive system has taken a rest. It's important not to overextend yourself, especially when your hunger comes back, and you're ravenous - which you will be.

During the reentry time, start by drinking fresh fruit juices. After that, begin to eat the fruit itself as well as milk and yogurt. Next, you may introduce salads and vegetables. Finally, as you reintroduce protein, it's best done with cheese, eggs, and nuts, adding fish and meat last of all.

Also, extended fasting is like a reset for your body. There may have been things you wanted to change about your diet and begin living a more healthy lifestyle. Don't go back to the same bad habits after the fast is over. You may have broken a sugar, fast food, or junk food addiction. Be wise about how you eat after you've reset your body with fasting.

Just because the fast has ended, that doesn't mean your dedication to prayer and God's Word have ended. Don't slip back into an undisciplined lifestyle. Continue to pray, study, and stay in a state of sensitivity to God's Spirit.

Paul wrote that he disciplined his body daily so that it wouldn't overtake him (1 Corinthians 9:27). Obviously, he wasn't fasting every day. He was making an effort to subdue his flesh. You should do the same.

WHAT ABOUT TAKING MY MEDICATION?

Some people want to fast but feel like they can't because of a sickness, disease, or prescribed medication they must take with food.

I want to stress that this book is not to be used as medical advice. I've never advised people to stop taking their medication "by faith."

I believe that God will heal you, your doctor will see the results of God's power, and take you off of your medication. Carolyn and I have seen this happen many times throughout our ministry.

If you're sick or taking medication, continue to believe the Lord to receive your healing. He loves you and doesn't want harm to come to you.

Furthermore, healing is one of the benefits that the Bible says accompanies fasting and prayer (Isaiah 58:8). If you choose to fast and pray while sick or on medication, ask the Lord to heal you as a testimony to his goodness and his power.

It may be wise to proceed with caution and begin with intermittent fasting. However, no matter what you do, never cease praying. Continue to spend time in the presence of God.

SHOULD I FAST IF I'M PREGNANT?

I believe that fasting while pregnant is a bad idea. Your baby is growing and continuously in need of nutrients and strength.

There is very little research available about the effects of fasting during pregnancy, but even intermittent fasting is generally discouraged.

Issues like iron deficiency anemia are more common in pregnant women. As a result, if a baby doesn't get enough iron—especially in the third trimester—they may be at higher risk of developing anemia before their first birthday.

When pregnant, you should continue to pray but focus on helping the baby gain weight, providing nutrition to help with brain and body development, and developing maternal fat stores if you plan to breastfeed.[1]

Don't feel guilty if everyone around you is on a corporate fast, and you're not able to participate because of your pregnancy. You'll have plenty of opportunities to fast during your life. God gave you that child as a gift from Heaven. Take care of it.

SHOULD MY CHILDREN FAST?

It's important to remember that children are still in their developmental stages. This is a critical time as they're growing, and they need proper nutrients as they do.

Most doctors discourage fasting for children before they hit puberty. They can be at risk of problems arising from fasting because their metabolisms are so high.

If your children are going to join you while fasting, the best solution may be the six to six fast, also known as the sunrise to sunset fast.

This way, they're still giving up meals and making a sacrifice to seek the Lord, but they're not missing a proper daily intake of nutrients.

The Lord understands your child's physical needs. After all, he created their bodies. Should the Lord give us more time on the earth, your children will have plenty of time to fast and pray as they get older.

WHAT CAN I DRINK WHEN I'M FASTING?

Without fail, anytime we begin a corporate fast, I get messages from people asking what they can have during the fast. Obviously, you won't be eating any food.

Usually, when we fast, we do a liquid-only fast. This usually includes, juice, broth, coffee, tea, and plenty of water (aim for two or three liters a day).

As fasting is a time to deny your flesh, I wouldn't recommend drinking soda or other drinks that are high in calories. You could drink three flavored lattes each day and still take in the same amount of calories as if you were eating meals. If you keep the purpose of fasting at the forefront with the goal of denying your flesh and seeking God, I believe you'll make the right choices.

HOW LONG SHOULD I FAST?

As I said in the chapter entitled *How Long Should I Fast and Pray?*, the Bible does not give us any instructions regarding how long we should fast.

However, I do have a few suggestions. First, you can't decide not to fast. Christ expects his followers to fast throughout their lives.

Second, unless you *truly* feel the Lord speak to you (and it better be something of life-or-death importance), don't fast for longer than forty days. It's the longest fast recorded in Scripture, and it was sufficient to prepare the Son of God for earthly ministry. Why do you need to fast for a longer period of time than Christ?

Furthermore, I don't necessarily think it's necessary for believers who aren't called into full-time ministry to fast for forty days. Although we have examples of the Apostle Paul fasting, we have no record that he ever fasted for longer than three days.

That brings me to my final suggestion. I would rather see believers engage in a dedicated three-day fast where they truly cut out all the excesses of life and seek the Lord in prayer than an extended fast done flippantly.

At that point, are you fasting to seek or please the Lord, or just to put another long-term fasting notch on your spiritual belt? A fast marked by time wasted on entertainment, little or no prayer, and Bible reading is a waste of that believer's time. He or she might as well have continued eating. Fasting is an important and solemn time between you and the Lord. Yes, it will produce spiritual joy, but it's not a vacation from life. Take it seriously, and you will experience the benefits that accompany biblical fasting.

SHOULD I KEEP MY FAST A SECRET?

A common concept taught among Christians is that you must keep your fast a total secret or risk losing your spiritual reward.

I've seen this take awkward turns in conversation and sometimes border on lying. This is a misrepresentation of what Jesus taught during his famous Sermon on the Mount.

> *And when you fast, do not look gloomy like the hypocrites, for they disfigure their faces that their fasting may be seen by others ... they have received their reward.*
> *Matthew 6:16 ESV*

In this passage, Jesus isn't swearing his followers to secrecy. He's making a point that you shouldn't parade your fasting around to gain the attention of others. It's a deadly form of pride, and it makes fasting and prayer worthless.

However, there may be times you have to explain why you're not eating. You don't have to be prideful or religious about it.

Also, there may be occasions when your church calls a corporate fast where everyone joins for a certain period of time. We often do this at the beginning of each year.

Obviously, during a corporate fast, everyone will be aware that the others are fasting. You're not forfeiting your reward in these instances.

The most important thing to remember is that you should never flaunt your fasting in front of others to look more holy or spiritual. That kind of pride *will* cause you to lose your reward.

WHAT IF I MESS UP? CAN I RESTART?

Anyone who has spent time fasting knows that we've all been in this position before. You set a goal to fast for a specific period of time—personally or corporately—but at some point, your flesh overcomes you, and you break your fast before your goal date.

Maybe your church is on a twenty-one day fast, or you decided to personally fast and pray for ten days, and you end up eating for one reason or another. As Jesus said regarding prayer, "The spirit indeed is willing, but the flesh is weak" (Matthew 26:41).

Usually, guilt sets in, and you feel like you've failed God. Don't allow this to cancel your fast altogether. Maybe you were only four days into your church's twenty-one day fast. Don't say, "Well, I failed. I'll try again next year."

Get right back on the fast! Start again from that moment. I don't mean that you should take your vows lightly and be flippant in fasting, but don't let one moment of weakness stop you from continuing in dedication to the Lord.

Ask the Lord to forgive you for not fulfilling your vow (Ecclesiastes 5:4-6), and get right back into his presence as quickly as possible.

SHOULD COUPLES NOT HAVE SEX DURING FASTS?

One question that arises from time to time is that of intimacy during times of fasting and prayer. The Apostle Paul wrote to the Corinthians about this very issue. He emphasized the importance of married couples making room for intimacy. As the husband has control of the wife's body, and the wife has control of her husband's body, there should never be sexual deprivation.

> *Do not deprive one another [of sex], except perhaps by agreement for a limited time, that you may devote yourselves to prayer; but then come together again, so that Satan may not tempt you because of your lack of self-control.*
> *1 Corinthians 7:5 ESV [Emphasis added]*

By inspiration of the Holy Spirit, Paul did make provision to pause sexual relations for a short period of time of devoted prayer, and that would include fasting.

However, notice that he said, "by agreement." That's a significant point when dealing with intimacy. It ensures that no one can use spiritual excuses to deprive their spouse of intimacy.

If your husband or wife doesn't agree with pausing intimacy, it should not be done. Your spouse has authority over your body (1 Corinthians 7:3-4).

SHOULD I EXERCISE DURING MY FAST?

Years ago, during my father's campmeeting in West Virginia, something strange happened that I'll never forget. It illustrates the answer to this question perfectly.

We were in the middle of a service, when suddenly, there was a loud crash in the middle of the sanctuary. An audible gasp swept through the room.

When I turned around to look, I saw the cameraman, who had been standing on a platform filming the service, sprawled out on the ground between the pews.

He had been on an extended fast but had not stopped working out. That morning he participated in a local marathon and ran over twenty miles.

Obviously, the exertion was too much for his body,

and he fainted and fell off the platform. Thankfully, he was okay.

It's important to remember that fasting is a time to separate yourself from your everyday routine and deny your flesh. I'm not saying you can't continue to work out if you're fasting for a shorter period of time, but during extended fasts, exercise isn't a good idea.

You're already severely limiting your caloric intake, and — if fasting properly — your blood sugar will be low. Burning additional calories isn't a good idea.

Exercise will also make you hungrier and increase the probability that you'll break your fast.

Let me also be very clear about an issue I see regarding Christians who work out and fasting. I've seen people who refuse to fast (and I mean truly fast the way the Bible describes) because they won't stop their workout routine.

They have to continue to take in protein, supplements and stay on their eating plan, so they don't compromise or lose their "gains."

Let me be very straightforward. If you refuse to engage in fasting and prayer because you don't want to interrupt your workout routine, exercise has become your god.

You're more concerned about how your body looks than obeying the Word of God. This is the exact opposite attitude we must have to fast and pray.

If you can't pause your workout regimen for three, seven, ten, or twenty-one days to seek the Lord, it has taken control of your life and become an idol to you. (See 2 Peter 2:19.)

WILL FASTING RUIN MY METABOLISM?

This is a legitimate concern for many people who are considering fasting. Some people believe that when you fast, your body enters "starvation mode," and your metabolism slows considerably, preventing you from burning fat in the future.

However, that's not true. In fact, even short-term fasts may increase your metabolic rate. Contrary to popular belief, eating more frequently doesn't increase your metabolic rate causing your body to burn more calories.[3]

ISN'T FASTING JUST ASCETICISM?

First, if you're unfamiliar with the word, let me define it. Asceticism is severe self-discipline and avoidance of all forms of indulgence, typically for religious reasons.

The easy answer to this question is, yes, in a way, fasting is asceticism. Jesus, the disciples, and any disciplined Christian could be called "ascetic."

However, throughout history asceticism began to develop into harmful error as it was practiced among other world religions. That's why the word now has a more negative connotation among Christians.

In *God's Chosen Fast*, Arthur Wallis wrote that we can break asceticism down into three stages throughout the Christian church's history.[4]

First would be biblical fasting as defined in this book. The motives are right, and the method is scriptural. This is good, and God is pleased with these actions.

Next was the renunciation of all physical comforts and regular social interaction as you would see with a hermit or a monk. This includes various forms of self-inflicted bodily torture such as wearing a cilice—a shirt made of coarse, animal hair, sometimes with the addition of sticks or thin, metal wires to mortify the body.

With the erroneous practice of medieval asceticism came false doctrine. There was a wrong view that God takes pleasure in pain, suffering, and hardship. Even today, some believe that the will of God must be the hardest path available.

The concept that man could acquire favor with God by acts of self-mortification led to the heretical doctrine of penance and the atoning for sins by indulgences.

Finally, the third stage of asceticism stems from the

misconception that the human body is evil and, there-fore, must be subjected to rigorous self-discipline in the extreme. Whatever the body wants must be taken from it in order to restrain its evil desires.

For example, does the body desire sexual activity? Take a vow of celibacy. Does it crave sleep? Develop a "night watch" so that when the bell tolls in the night, monks must rise from their sleep to participate in a prayer vigil. Does the body crave comfort? Let it be subjected to all kinds of hardship, even tortured for its many sins. These can all be seen historically within the monastic system.

While fasting is a form of denying self, those who fear the extremes of secular asceticism have backed away from the biblical expectation of fasting.

Don't throw the baby out with the bath water. There are extremes in every area of life, but they don't negate the genuine principle from which they're derived.

Never let an uninformed person make you feel bad for fasting by making you think it's an arbitrary, man-made, ascetic principle.

Chapter Twelve
SPIRITUAL BENEFITS OF FASTING

Unlike fasting for health purposes or fasts done by other religions, biblical fasting has spiritual benefits. We are fasting and praying in service of the only true and living God. When we seek him, he answers us.

God spoke through the prophet Isaiah to the people of Israel and gave them instructions about fasting and prayer and then outlined the supernatural benefits that would result from their obedience.

As we take a closer look at what God said in Isaiah chapter 58, we'll see that there are distinct blessings that are released when we engage his presence in fasting and prayer. Let's look at the scriptures describing God's chosen fast and then examine the benefits that come from our obedience.

Is this not the fast that I have chosen: To loose the bonds of wickedness, To undo the heavy burdens, To let the oppressed go free, And that you break every yoke? Then your light shall break forth like the morning, Your healing shall spring forth speedily, And your righteousness shall go before you; The glory of the Lord shall be your rear guard. Then you shall call, and the Lord will answer.

Isaiah 58:6,8,9 NKJV

Before we continue, it's also important to note that God was unhappy with their fasting. He considered it empty of meaning because of how they were conducting themselves as they were calling out to him.

"Why don't you notice when we fast?" They asked God. "Why don't you pay attention when we humble ourselves?"

"Look," God replied, "At the same time you fast, you satisfy your selfish desires, you oppress your workers. Look, your fasting is accompanied by arguments, brawls, and fistfights. Is this really the kind of fasting I want?" (See Isaiah 58:3-5 NET.)

This is similar to what Jesus was condemning among the Pharisees in Matthew chapter 6. God is displeased with empty dedication when our other actions don't reflect God's desires.

We can't trick God with disingenuous service. He knows the very thoughts and intentions of our hearts. As the Bible says, "No creature is hidden from his sight, but all are naked and exposed to the eyes of him to whom we must give account" (Hebrews 4:13).

Always make sure that your actions match the state of your heart. God won't be satisfied with mere lip service or religious rituals.

As you truly judge and humble yourself before the Lord, you will provoke his favor. God promised the following benefits would follow *true* fasting.

1. FRESH REVELATION AND FAVOR

"Then your light will break forth like the morning," God promised. Many times, when the Bible speaks of light, it is speaking of revelation knowledge. Divine understanding of God's Word sets us on another level in the supernatural realm.

David said that God's Word became a lamp for his feet and a light unto his path (Psalm 119:105). Your level of understanding of God's Word determines the level of freedom you will experience in life. The truth you know will set you free (John 8:32).

The path of your life becomes illuminated by your revelation and understanding of the Scripture.

I remember the first time I ever experienced this explosion of revelation in my life. I was fasting, praying, had set aside time to hear from God, and read his Word. I grabbed my notebook and pen and sat down in my office. I began by praying and thanking God that he was opening the eyes of my understanding as I read.

I opened my Bible expecting to read John chapters 1 through 9 in the time that I had allotted for myself to study.

As I read through John chapter 1, God began to release revelation that I never had before. I furiously scribbled notes in my journal. When I finally looked down at my watch as I prepared to move on to chapter 2, I was surprised to find that I had spent my entire allotted time — one hour — in just one chapter.

I had made almost four pages of notes on just one chapter of the Bible. What happened? *My light broke forth like the morning.*

The first benefit of fasting and prayer that God promised is that you will gain an unnatural understanding of his Word. This one aspect of fasting and prayer opens a whole new world of possibilities to you as a follower of Christ.

That doesn't mean the Lord can't show you things

when you're not fasting, but with your flesh subdued, that "carnal filter" isn't operating. Silencing the flesh is necessary. As Job said, "Teach me, and I will be silent; make me understand how I have gone astray" (Job 6:24).

When Elijah was in the midst of depression and anxiety, the Lord encouraged him and spoke to him. But look at how it happened.

Elijah was staying in a cave and the Lord told him to go stand on the mountain before him. When he did, the Lord passed by. First, there was a strong wind that tore the mountains, but God wasn't in it.

Next, there was an earthquake, but the Lord wasn't in it. Following the earthquake, there was a fire, but the Lord wasn't in the fire. Finally, after the fire, there was a whisper. Only then was the Lord speaking to him (1 Kings 19:9-13).

Many times, we think the Lord only moves in demonstrative, in-your-face ways. Often, however, God is speaking quietly.

If we don't humble ourselves and quiet the flesh, we could miss it. We're required to draw near to God *before* he draws near to us. (See James 4:8.)

In the context of Isaiah's passage, light is referring to the favor of God that would return to his people. True fasting and prayer provokes the favor of God. Notice what the Psalmist wrote concerning the favor of God. I find it interesting that he refers to God as "a sun" referring to the favor of his light.

> *For the LORD God is a sun and shield;*
> *the LORD bestows favor and honor. No*
> *good thing does he withhold from those*
> *who walk uprightly.*
> **Psalm 84:11 ESV**

When God shines upon you, his favor will be evident in your life. When Moses pronounced the generational blessing upon Aaron and his sons, he used the phrase, "The Lord make his face to shine upon you and be gracious to you" (Numbers 6:25).

In his commentary on Numbers, German scholar, Martin Noth, rightly describes this image of a shining face as "a figure of speech for benevolence and favour."[1]

When we humble ourselves before the Lord, he will exalt us (1 Peter 5:6). The Word of God promises us that if we will humble ourselves it will attract more favor from the Lord. (James 4:6; Proverbs 3:34).

Without question, fasting and prayer will provoke God's interaction and attract his favor to your life.

2. EXPEDITED HEALING

The second thing clearly promised as a benefit of fasting and prayer is that divine healing will quickly manifest in your body.

Wait a minute, I can hear some of you thinking. *Healing was purchased for us by the blood of Jesus on the cross. Why should we have to do anything else to receive it?*

This is a common question that many believers have. While the combination of fasting and prayer is not the only way that believers may receive healing from God, it is one avenue given to us to activate that blessing.

One thing we must understand about redemption is that it is not a package of promises, rather, it is a collection of covenant terms.

More simply, none of the blessings we receive from God come to us automatically. Each one must be received and appropriated by faith.

If God's blessings were automatic then Jesus' death alone would have set the world right with God. There would be no more sinners left on the earth and we could all go directly to Heaven.

However, Jesus' death was only God's half of the covenant transaction. Now, if we want to receive salvation, we also have a part to play.

The Bible says that we must confess that Jesus is Lord

and believe in our heart that God raised Him from the dead. That is our response to God that completes the transaction of salvation (Romans 10:9). Without that action of faith, we are not entitled to salvation.

In the same way, God gave us a covenant of financial blessing in redemption (2 Corinthians 8:9). Does that mean that all Christians are wealthy and have no needs? Absolutely not.

Until our half of the covenant is activated, we have no right to obtain financial blessing (Luke 6:38).

You can readily see that any blessing God has provided for his children must be obtained by faith. Just like the laying on of hands, anointing with oil, and prayer cloths, fasting and prayer are just another avenue to receive divine healing.

Our healing, like any other aspect of the covenant, must be received and activated by forceful faith.

God created our bodies and knows more about them than any doctor or specialist on the earth.

Though fasting is an action of faith and obedience, God also understands the need for our bodies to be cleansed from the harmful toxins that pass through it on a regular basis.

Tests have proven that the average American consumes and assimilates four pounds of chemical preservatives, coloring, stabilizers, flavorings, and other additives each year. These build up in our bodies and cause illness and disease.

Periodic fasts are necessary to flush out the poisons. Fasting gives your body time to heal itself. It relieves tension and gives your digestive system a rest. Fasting lowers your blood pressure and can lower your cholesterol.[2]

We covered the natural benefits of fasting in depth in the chapter entitled, *"What Will Fasting Do To My Body?"*

Jentezen Franklin, who has authored multiple books, articles, and many sermons on the subject of fasting concludes, "Fasting slows your aging process. Moses fasted often, including two forty-day fasts, and the Bible says in Deuteronomy 34:7, 'Moses was one hundred and twenty years old when he died. His eyes were not dim nor his natural vigor diminished.'"[3]

Without a doubt, God knew fasting had natural benefits as well as spiritual ones when He commanded his children to engage in it. Fasting and prayer allow you to take action and obtain from God what belongs to you through your covenant with Jesus.

3. OBSTACLES REMOVED

Native Americans have made up an integral part of U.S. military conflicts since America's beginning.

Colonists recruited Native American allies during

such instances as the Pequot War, the Revolutionary War, as well as in the War of 1812.

Native Americans also fought on both sides during the American Civil War, as well as military missions abroad including the most notable, the Codetalkers who served in World War II.[4]

The Indian scouts were a fast-moving, aggressive, and knowledgeable asset to the U.S. army. They often proved to be immune to army notions of discipline and demeanor, but they proved expert in traversing the vast distances of the American West and providing intelligence — and often a shock force — to the soldiers who sought hostile Indians.

One chief scout, Stanton G. Fisher, emphasized the importance of Native American Scouts by saying of the soldiers, "Uncle Sam's boys are too slow for this business"[5]

The job of the scouts was to move ahead of the army and gather intelligence about what was ahead and if possible clear the way for the forces behind them.

In the same way that Fisher realized the U.S. military needed the assistance of the Native American Scouts because they were ill-equipped to handle the conditions they faced, believers need supernatural assistance to successfully navigate our purpose and call.

This benefit is supernaturally afforded to us through fasting and prayer. The prophet Jeremiah declared that the Lord is our righteousness (Jeremiah 23:6).

This means that the Lord will go ahead of us and prepare the way, warn us of things to come, and fight on our behalf.

A perfect picture of this principle is when the Lord spoke to King Cyrus through the prophet Isaiah. He assured him of success when he said:

> *I will go before you, Cyrus, and level the*
> *mountains. I will smash down gates of*
> *bronze and cut through bars of iron. And*
> *I will give you treasures hidden in the*
> *darkness — secret riches.*
>
> *Isaiah 45:2-3 NLT*

Every hindrance that stands in your way will be leveled by the power of God. One translation of this passage says that God will, "make the crooked places straight." This has special significance because when your path is crooked, it slows your momentum.

Think about it, anytime there is a race that measures how fast someone or something is, it's conducted in a straight line. Whether it's the 100-yard dash or a car company calculating how quickly their new vehicle accelerates from 0-60 miles per hour.

When you have to make turns or avoid obstacles, you

always have to slow down and lose momentum. I'm always frustrated watching the skiing event in the Olympics where the participant has to ski way out around the flags as they come down the mountain. It takes too long. Of course, this is coming from the guy who likes to go to the very top of the steepest hill, tuck my poles under my arms and go down the mountain as fast as I can.

God wants you to be able to run your Christian race with power and momentum. It's the enemy who wants to slow you down and put obstacles in your path.

When the Lord goes before you, he won't just remove hindrances from your path, he will connect you with the people that he has called you to help and those who will help you.

THE FAST THAT BROUGHT
COLONEL SANDERS TO JESUS

Pastor Waymon Rodgers, who founded the 9,000-member Evangel World Prayer Center in Louisville, Kentucky, was a man of prayer and fasting.

In the mid-1970s he was fasting, praying, and asking God to bring revival to their church. God answered his prayer and a 17-week revival broke out.

During the revival, someone had the courage to walk up to Kentucky Fried Chicken founder Colonel Harland

Sanders on the street, and with just a friendly word, invited him to attend special evangelistic services, and to hear good singing. Pastor Rodgers remembers how it happened:

> I saw him come in. You couldn't miss him in a crowd, with his white suit and his identifying white beard and full head of hair. I knew God was going to do something special that night. I felt it immediately. Our people had been praying.
>
> As our evangelist moved into the service, I left the platform and sat with the Colonel on the front pew. The invitation began. He raised his hand for prayer. There were tears. I said, "Colonel, let's get down on our knees and talk to God."
>
> "I don't know what to say," he replied.
>
> "Let's start with the sinner's prayer," I suggested.
>
> "God be merciful to me, a sinner," the Colonel said.' [I] will always remember how the Colonel's problem tumbled out. A stain, stubborn and shameful, had fastened itself to this proud, successful man's life. He wanted to be free from cursing, which festered his ordinary conversation. He was never free from it. It made him feel as rotten as liquor does a drunkard. It was the one bad thing he had learned to do during his

years of railroading. It marked him.

He had tried in vain to break the habit. This was proof enough that he was not saved, no matter how often he attended church.

Suddenly the Colonel lifted his head. He looked at me and told me that it was the first time he had ever experienced the presence of Christ within his heart. A moment or two later, I suggested that we talk to God together about his problem of cursing.

He said, "Pastor Rodgers, we don't need to do that. Christ has done that for me already."[6]

Not long after Colonel Sanders' conversion, he gave a $1 million offering to the church. This was also an answer to Pastor Rodgers' fasting and prayer, and it was a great testimony as God had increased the church so steadily that they had to build a larger building.

Fasting and prayer cause the power of God to go before you and prepare the way for your glorious destiny.

4. DIVINE PROTECTION

I've heard it said that the elements of the Armor of God, which are described in detail in Ephesians chapter 6, are designed to only cover the front of the believer. The reasoning behind this statement is that "God never expects his soldiers to retreat from their enemy."

While this point might elicit shouting and dancing during a sermon on the victorious church, I've always found the argument a bit thin.

I find it hard to believe that God would protect us from the front, but fail to protect us from behind.

Isaiah 58 clearly shows us that through fasting and prayer, the glory of God becomes our rear guard. He protects us from behind no matter what our enemy may have planned to destroy us.

It's a wonderful thing to know that God's got your back. He never wants to see us fail, but many times we're so busy with the details of life that we don't hear his voice, or we don't petition him by faith to receive secrets about the future (Jeremiah 33:3).

Remember, everything we receive from God must be received by faith. If actions of faith are not present, there is nothing to motivate God to move on our behalf.

Prayer and fasting are faith actions that motivate God to reveal hidden things regarding our future. According to the book of James, one of the main reasons we don't have what God has prepared for us is because we fail to ask him for it (James 4:3).

The Bible is very clear about God's divine protection working on behalf of his people.

*No weapon turned against you will suc-
ceed. You will silence every voice raised
up to accuse you. These benefits are en-
joyed by the servants of the Lord; their
vindication will come from me. I, the
Lord, have spoken!*

Isaiah 54:17 NLT

When we serve the Lord, we enjoy these benefits. You
don't have to be afraid of the sneak attack your enemy is
planning against you. There are no "terrors of the night"
that can overtake you (Psalm 91:5). Fasting and prayer
empower you to be guarded on every side by the glory
of the most high God.

5. EXPEDITED ANSWERS TO PRAYER

One of the wonderful aspects of prayer coupled with
fasting that we see throughout the God's Word, is that it
expedites the answers to our prayers.

While we as New Testament believers may not need
to fast to have our prayers answered, there is no question
that fasting is a powerful supplement to our prayers.

Sadly, many Christians don't pray as often or as diligently as God would like. This is a major roadblock that
causes them to be stuck at a certain point in their pur-

pose for an extended period of time allowing stagnation to set in.

One thing fasting definitely accomplishes for us is it keeps us in the mindset and atmosphere of prayer throughout our day. It weakens the flesh giving way to the desires of the spirit.

It's important to understand that God doesn't reward every believer. He rewards those who diligently seek him (Hebrews 11:6).

Fasting and prayer are undeniable access points into the presence of God, and proof that you are seeking him diligently. God spoke to the prophet Jeremiah and said:

> *And you will seek Me and find Me, when*
> *you search for Me with all your heart. I*
> *will be found by you, says the Lord.*
> *Jeremiah 29:13-14 NKJV*

In his definitive book on fasting, *God's Chosen Fast*, Arthur Wallis writes, "When a man is willing to set aside the legitimate appetites of the body to concentrate on the work of praying, he is demonstrating that he means business, that he is seeking with all his heart, and will not let God go unless he answers."[7]

Jesus explained to his disciples that there are different levels of supernatural opposition. When they failed to conquer a case of demonic possession, they were confused at their lack of results. Jesus explained that fasting and prayer are necessary to prevail against certain types of spiritual adversary (Mark 9:17-29).

My cousin, Jessica, and her husband, Steve, pastor a church in Montreal, Quebec. The church had purchased and met in a building that wasn't yet zoned for church gatherings. You can only apply for a zoning permit after you own a building.

However, an official on the city council told them, "As long as I'm here, you're not getting the permit."

Furthermore, as the church grew, they needed to build a new sanctuary, but they couldn't begin construction because they had been denied a zoning permit.

The church launched into twenty-one days of fasting and prayer. On the final day of the fast, corruption was discovered on the city council. The official who was opposing them was removed and replaced.

To further solidify their position, the Supreme Court of Quebec ruled that the city's practice of only allowing zoning for houses of worship in certain sections of the city was discriminatory, likening it to the ghettoization of the past.

This ruling set a precedent that not only brought victory to their church, but all churches to come.

The city worked willingly with the church, and they

SPIRITUAL BENEFITS OF FASTING

continued to expand by the power of God. Fasting and prayer bring quick answers and produce powerful breakthroughs.

If you've experienced a delay regarding something for which you've been believing, fast and pray!

6. DIVINE DIRECTION

I can remember the first time I ever saw my wife. I was in the middle of a Sunday-morning service at Dominion Christian Center where I was on staff.

I was leading praise and worship from behind the keyboard when the back doors opened and the most beautiful girl I'd ever seen walked in.

I was immediately smitten. I had to keep myself from glancing over at her throughout the whole service.

After we met and got to know each other, I realized that I really liked her. However, as an associate pastor, you can't just flippantly date girls in the church. If it was God's will for us to be together, I wanted to know beforehand so that no time was wasted.

I decided to fast and pray for three days — from Good Friday to Easter Sunday. I wanted a green light from the Holy Ghost. If I didn't get it, I made up my mind I would just move on and forget it.

After the morning service on Sunday, I went back to

my room and continued to pray. I felt the Lord tell me that she was the one for me.

I was very excited. I immediately sent a text asking her if she wanted to go on a date that night. I picked her up from work and we went to dinner together.

Afterward, as we were driving to her parent's house, I began to describe what I felt would be the future of our relationship.

I was confident that the Lord had spoken to me. Being called into full-time ministry is a serious thing. If the Lord didn't call her, too, there was no point in us being together.

I don't recommend that everyone lay all their cards on the table during the first date like I did. It could go sideways on you. Best case scenario, you may never hear from your date again, worst case scenario, you'll get slapped . . . and then never hear from them again.

On our first date, I told her that I loved her, that I believed we'd be married, have children, and minister together. I waited for her to open the door and run — but she didn't.

"I know," she said, and smiled. In the same way the Lord was guiding me, he was guiding her.

Divine direction is one of the main reasons God's people fasted in the Old and New Testament. They depended on hearing his voice.

*Then shall your light rise in the darkness
and your gloom be as the noonday. And
the LORD will guide you continually*
                    Isaiah 58:10-11 ESV

Divine direction is a vital resource for every believer. The outcome of your life will be very different when you follow the leading of the Lord.

In what is probably one of the most famous passages of Scripture, Psalm 23, David outlines the benefits that accompany being led by the Great Shepherd.

No lack in places of abundance, peace, restoration, proper direction and right paths, protection from evil, provision in the midst of enemies, fresh anointing, over-flow, goodness and mercy, and an eternal place in God's presence. That's what divine direction yields.

7. SUPERNATURAL STRENGTH

People often ask me, "How do you and your family travel all the time and go to revival night after night? Aren't you exhausted?"

We're not exhausted; we're refreshed. The only time I've ever been close to exhaustion is when I was doing things the Lord never led me to do.

Strength is afforded to those who seek the Lord in

fasting and prayer. In Isaiah 58:11, God promised to "Make your bones strong."

You would think that fasting would make you weaker, however, when your spirit becomes strong, it affects your entire being. Though some see it as a greeting, I believe John's words in the opening of his letter to Gaius illustrate a principle that remains true for all believers.

> *Beloved, I pray that you may prosper in all things and be in health, just as your soul prospers.*
>
> *3 John 1:2 NKJV*

Notice that soul prosperity seems to be the principle thing. Your life is governed by the issues that flow from your heart (Proverbs 4:23). The inner man can directly affect the outer man. For example, supernatural joy can produce strength and healing to your body (See Proverbs 17:22.) Similarly, Isaiah wrote:

> *But they who wait for the LORD shall renew their strength; they shall mount up with wings like eagles; they shall run and not be weary; they shall walk and not faint.*
>
> *Isaiah 40:31 ESV*

Fasting and prayer are one of the most direct ways to wait upon the Lord. In the New Testament, the prophetess, Anna, was *serving* the Lord in fasting and prayer. (See Luke 2:37.)

The life of Christ is one of the clearest pictures of fasting and prayer producing supernatural strength. After he was filled with the Spirit at the Jordan River, the Bible says he was led by the Spirit into the wilderness. That's where he spent forty days in fasting and prayer. The result?

> *And Jesus returned in the power of the Spirit to Galilee, and a report about him went out through all the surrounding country.*
>
> *Luke 4:14 ESV*

He returned in *power*. Though Jesus was the Son of God from the moment of birth, he produced no miracles until he was filled with the Spirit and he fasted and prayed. As soon as he returned, his miracles began. He was operating in supernatural strength.

8. VICTORY OVER TEMPTATION

While Christ was in the wilderness, he was tempted by the devil. Though he was, he never yielded to temptation one time. In the end, Satan had to flee from him because of his response to each temptation. Jesus understood the power of fasting and prayer. He knew that it would prepare him to overcome every temptation.

Later, he taught his disciples the same principle. The flesh must be subdued if we're going to be victorious whenever temptation arises. After waking his disciples from sleep when they should have been praying, he said to them:

> *Watch and pray that you may not enter into temptation. The spirit indeed is willing, but the flesh is weak.*
>
> *Matthew 26:41 ESV*

As I've covered throughout this book, the flesh must be subdued in order to please the Lord. The carnal nature of your flesh opposes the desires of the Spirit. (See Galatians 5:17.)

Freedom from sin—holiness—is such a powerful benefit because it unlocks all of the blessings of God. Pastor Enoch Adeboye once preached a message on holiness entitled *The Master Key.*

He taught that although there are many keys in the Bible, there is only one master key. A master key, he explained, can open any door.

While there are other keys in Scripture, there are ca-veats that can hinder them from working. For example, prayer is a key, but prayer can be hindered by unbelief, being double minded, or not walking in love.

The same is true about other biblical keys. Holiness, however, is the master key. There is nothing that can stop it, and no door it will not open.

> *For the LORD God is our sun and our shield. He gives us grace and glory. The LORD will withhold no good thing from those who do what is right.*
> *Psalm 84:11 NLT*

The ability to subdue your flesh, be led by the Spirit, and overcome temptation may be the greatest benefit of fasting and prayer that there is.

A preacher once asked, "What is the number one re-sponsibility of every believer?"

"To win the lost," someone answered him.

"No," he said. "Your number one responsibility is to make sure that *you* end up in Heaven."

Paul made this exact same distinction in his first let-ter to the Corinthians. He knew that his work wasn't as important as his eternal destination.

He responsibly subdued his body on a daily basis.

If he didn't, he could have preached to others and converted thousands into the kingdom of God but still been disqualified at the end of his life (1 Corinthians 9:27). Remember, God is the only boss who will fire you and let you keep on working.

As you fast and pray, you're putting yourself in position to live a life that's continually pleasing to the Lord, and by doing so, you will provoke his favor.

Chapter Thirteen

100 PRAYER POINTS TO BOOST YOUR DEVOTIONS

Have you ever wanted to pray for an extended period of time, but after you prayed for about five or ten minutes, you've said everything you can think to pray?

Maybe you've read portions of this book where I reference praying for an hour or longer, and you wonder how anyone could have that much to say in prayer.

I remember when I first began trying to spend more time praying. I'd pray for about ten to fifteen minutes and then have to spend the rest of the time praying in tongues because I'd run out of content.

When I first discovered Bishop David Oyedepo's and Pastor Enoch Adeboye's ministries and saw how they led corporate prayer, it was revelatory to me.

Throughout this book, I've referred to prayer points

that our ministry provides to help you get started in prayer. It was their ministries that introduced me to the concept of prayer points.

Don't be wary. This isn't some form of traditional prayer book or set of prayers you must methodically recite; these represent a beginning point to kickstart your prayer time.

As I mentioned, we provide Scripture references with each prayer point so that you have verses to stand on as you pray. Some will be praise, worship, and thanksgiving, others will be personal petitions, and some will be what I've referred to as "kingdom agenda prayers."

I know that these prayer points will build your faith and stir your spirit to go deeper in prayer than ever before. May you be incredibly blessed.

•   •   •

1. Thank the Lord that his mercies are new every morning in your life. [Lamentations 3:22-23]

2. Thank God that he is keeping us in perfect peace because our minds are stayed on him. [Isaiah 26:3]

3. Thank God that his glory is manifesting all over the earth. [Psalm 19:1-4]

4. Thank God for preserving our lives from all evil everywhere we go. [Psalm 121:1-8]

5. Thank God that he will show himself mighty on our behalf because his eyes will find our hearts turned toward him. [2 Chronicles 16:9]

6. Praise God that we will see his mighty acts in our lives and in this ministry this month and throughout the year. [Psalm 150:2]

7. Put a new song of praise in my mouth today that will cause people to see Christ in me. [Psalm 40:3]

8. As I praise You today, fill my mouth with laughter and my tongue with singing. [Psalm 126:2]

9. As I praise You today, fill me with supernatural strength to accomplish my purpose. [Nehemiah 8:10]

10. Praise God that all your requests will be supernaturally granted because his hand is on your life. [Nehemiah 2:8 / Ezra 7:6]

11. Give me an overwhelming desire to live for you with all my heart. [Matthew 5:6 / Psalm 51:10]

12. Thank and praise God for his true ministers all over the earth. [Ephesians 4:11-13]

13. Thank God for fighting in your country against destruction and terrorists. [Psalm 35:18-27 / 3:7]

14. Thank God that this year's fruit will be greater than last year's because of your supernatural dedication to God's kingdom. [John 15:5]

15. Ask God to make you worthy to receive his divine promotion this year and every year. [Psalm 75:6-7]

16. Thank God that he is securely establishing you in his kingdom forever. [Psalm 40:2]

17. Thank God that we will steadily increase in every area until the coming of Christ. [Proverbs 4:18]

18. Ask God to keep you in supernatural humility for the rest of your days. [Matthew 5:5]

19. Thank God that supernatural humility will cause you to have favor with men and be exceedingly great. [Numbers 12:3 / Exodus 11:3 / Matthew 5:5]

20. Praise God for his Word that has been exalted above his name. [Psalm 138:2]

21. Praise God that his Word is imparting health and strength to your entire being. [Proverbs 4:20-22]

22. Praise God that his Word is making your ways prosperous and causing you to succeed in all you do. [Joshua 1:8]

23. Praise God that his Word over your life is operating in full strength and will accomplish his purpose in you. [Isaiah 55:11]

24. Praise God that his Word is penetrating your life and judging the thoughts and intentions of your heart. [Hebrews 4:12]

25. Thank God for sending his Word to heal you and deliver you from all destruction. [Psalm 107:20 / John 1:14]

26. Praise God that there is no plot or plan of the enemy that could ever succeed against your life or ministry. [Isaiah 54:17]

27. Ask God to remove every enemy who would seek to hinder your purpose and call. [Acts 13:6-12]

28. Ask God to arise in your life and scatter his enemies in our nations, our churches, our families and our ministries. [Psalm 68:1]

29. Ask God to cause every power of the enemy at work in your life to become impotent by his mighty power. [Psalm 68:2]

30. Ask God to arise and cause all those against the church and the kingdom of God to be completely frustrated in their operations. [Psalm 68:1 / Matthew 16:18]

31. Ask God to supernaturally drive wickedness from your home. [Psalm 68:2]

32. Ask God to drive wicked people who seek to destroy you away from your home, family, life and ministry. [Psalm 68:2]

33. Thank you Lord for protecting your church (people and properties) from the aggression of destroyers. [Psalm 91:1-16]

34. Ask God to stretch forth his hand and subdue every demonic and carnal personality rising against your purpose and ministry. [Isaiah 45:1]

35. Ask God to go before you and destroy anything that would waste your time or delay you in your purpose. [Isaiah 45:2]

36. Thank God that no matter what season the earth is in, you will consistently bear fruit for his kingdom. [Psalm 1:3]

37. Thank God that because of your righteous dedication you will never be weakened, downsized or withered. [Psalm 1:3]

38. Thank God that everything you set your hand to do will prosper because of your righteous dedication. [Psalm 1:3 / Deuteronomy 28:8]

39. Ask God to divide the light from the darkness and expose any activity of the enemy in our churches, ministries, homes and lives. [Genesis 1:4]

40. Ask God to perform creative miracles in our churches, ministries, homes and lives. [John 9:1-7]

41. Ask God to continue to be the Shepherd of your soul. [Psalm 23:1]

42. Ask God to give us a heart to obey him as sheep obey the shepherd. [Psalm 23:1]

43. Thank him that because of his leading, you will never lack for anything. [Psalm 23:1]

44. Praise God that he prepared a table for you, a peaceful refreshing and nourishment, in the presence of your enemies and those who would seek to destroy you. [Psalm 23:5]

45. Praise God that his goodness and mercy have been assigned to your life for the rest of eternity. [Psalm 23:6]

46. Thank God that his right hand is holding you up in strength. [Psalm 63:8]

47. Thank God that your righteous dedication ensures that his ears are open to your prayers. [1 Peter 3:12]

48. Thank God that your righteous dedication ensures that his eyes are watching over you. [1 Peter 3:12]

49. Father, as you are holy, keep us in your holiness. [1 Peter 1:16]

50. Holy Spirit, supernaturally empower us to live in the perfection of our heavenly Father. [Matthew 5:48]

51. Ask God for the grace to walk circumspectly before him. [Genesis 17:1]

52. Thank God for the mighty baptism of the Holy Spirit in your life. [Acts 2:1-4]

53. Praise God for Holy Spirit's power to produce signs and wonders for the kingdom of Heaven. [Acts 1:8]

54. God, give us supernatural boldness and utterance to proclaim the gospel of Christ. [Ephesians 6:18]

55. Father, help us to win an unprecedented number of souls for your kingdom. [Matthew 9:37-38]

56. Father, give us supernatural wisdom to walk in your purpose. [James 1:5]

57. Father, give me supernatural ability to live in wisdom, constantly understand your will, and make the

most of every opportunity. [Ephesians 5:15-16]

58. Father, open the eyes of my understanding and show me secrets about the future. [Jeremiah 33:3]

59. Thank you, Father, that through your omniscient power you answer before I call unto to you. [Isaiah 65:24]

60. Thank you, Father, that you will never delay to hear my prayers. [Isaiah 65:24]

61. I thank You, Father, that the cares of this world will never enter my life, home or ministry ever again from this day forward. [Psalm 23:2]

62. I praise you, Father, for granting me a supernatural peace that passes human understanding. [Philippians 4:7]

63. Pray for the president, king, or prime minister of your nation, and his or her cabinet. [1 Timothy 2:1-4]

64. Father, we pray for the salvation of the souls of politicians and leaders in our nation. [1 Timothy 2:1-4]

65. We pray that our nation will be exalted because of the righteous who inhabit it. [Proverbs 14:34]

66. We pray against natural disasters in our nation. [Psalm 91:3]

67. No road accident, plane crash, or shipwreck will befall me as God's child and servant. [Psalm 91]

68. As God's children, we will complete our race and we will not be overtaken by any sudden death. [Psalm 91:7-8 / 2 Timothy 4:7]

69. Our bodies are divinely protected and will not be broken. [Psalm 34:20]

70. No damage will touch our properties or possessions this year in Jesus' mighty name. [Psalm 91:1 / Malachi 3:11-12]

71. Thank you, Father, that no evil spirit at work against my life, home, or ministry will be able to stay hidden. It will be revealed and cast out in Jesus' name. [Mark 5:1-20]

72. God, we ask you to cage and disgrace every Sanbal-

lat and Tobiah assigned from hell to hinder the work you have called us to do. [Nehemiah 4:4]

73. As our ways please you, Lord, may we spend our days in prosperity and our years in pleasures. [Job 36:11]

74. As we honor you with our lives and finances, open the windows of Heaven and pour us out a blessing we don't have room to contain. [Malachi 3:10]

75. God, condemn any tongue that rises against us as we work for you. Silence every voice that would attempt to bring judgement against us. [Isaiah 54:17]

76. We ask you to supernaturally make available what was previously unavailable, do the impossible and open closed doors this year. [Exodus 14:19-26]

77. We praise you, God, that we will always be the head and never the tail, always ending on top and never at the bottom. [Deuteronomy 28:13]

78. Ask God to send men and women of like faith into your life to strengthen you, and you them so that you may run with momentum. [Proverbs 27:17]

79. Ask God to remove every relationship from your life that is pulling you away from his plan, call and purpose for you. [2 Corinthians 6:14-18]

80. God, we ask you to open the doors for the gospel to be preached in the unreached nations and regions of the earth. [Matthew 24:14]

81. God, we ask you to destroy fraud and corruption in our nation and the states in which we live. [Psalm 1:4-5]

82. God, we ask you to let us do *nothing* except what you have mandated. Let us go *nowhere* that you have not commissioned us, and let us *never have* what you have not prepared for us to have. [Psalm 127:1]

83. Thank and Praise God that no matter the condition of the global economy, his children will always have plenty, be satisfied, and never be ashamed. [Joel 2:26]

84. Let us never trust in the strength of men. Our help comes only from the Lord. [Psalm 121:2]

85. Let us see the hand of God in supernatural assistance this year. [Psalm 60:11]

86. Ask God for help in any area in which you may need help. [Psalm 108:12]

87. Pray that God gives you supernatural endurance to finish your race in his kingdom. [Matthew 24:10-13]

88. Ask God to revive every believer who has grown cold and blow his breath into them so they may live in the fire of the Holy Ghost again. [Ezekiel 37:4-6]

89. Ask God to reverse the irreversible in your nation. [Psalm 125:3]

90. Let our testimonies be so intense this year that even the heathen will testify on our behalf that the hand of God is on our lives. [Psalm 126:2]

91. Ask God to restore to you every year that was eaten by the locust. [Joel 2:25]

92. Thank God that you will not know sickness in any form again from this day forward. [1 Peter 2:24]

93. Ask God to cause your cup to overflow with the very best you can have this year. [Psalm 23:5]

94. Ask God to make you a blessing to the entire world. [Genesis 12:2-3]

95. Ask God to keep you in purity and empower you to forsake every temptation. [Matthew 26:41]

96. Ask God to put an end to every one of your problems this year. [Psalm 34:19]

97. Ask God to use you this year to deliver men from every oppression of the devil. [Acts 10:38]

98. Ask God to part every river in your life and remove everything that is blocking the way to your destiny. [2 Kings 2:12-13 / Matthew 7:7]

99. Thank God that you will walk in supernatural joy for the rest of your life, and that depression, anxiety and panic will be kept far from you. [Psalm 16:11]

100. Ask God to give us unhindered access to his ways and his thoughts this year. [Isaiah 55:9]

ACKNOWLEDGMENTS

Thank you, Lord.

Thank you, Dad and Mom.

Thank you, Carolyn.

Thank you, Uncle Terry.

Thank you, Tiffany Farley.

Thank you, Victory Tribe.

NOTES

10 REASONS TO FAST AND PRAY

1. Sinek, Simon. Start with Why: How Great Leaders Inspire Everyone to Take Action. Portfolio Penguin, 2019.Potts, John. "The Roots of Charisma." SpringerLink, Palgrave Macmillan, London, 1 Jan. 1970, link.springer.com/chapter/10.1057% 2F9780230244832_2.

2. Kai-man, Ip. An Interview with Grandmaster Yip Man, Martial Hero Magazine, 2014, www.kwokwingchun.com/about-wing-chun/ip-mans-wing-chun/interview--with-grandmaster-yip-man/.

3. Piper, John. A Hunger for God: Desiring God Through Fasting and Prayer. Crossway, 2013.

4. "Chapter 1: The Price of God's Miracle Working Power." The Price of God's Miracle Working Power, by A. A. Allen, Schambach Revivals Inc., 1991, pp. 17–18.

THE SUPERNATURAL POWER OF SELF-DENIAL

1. The Price of God's Miracle Working Power (p. 66-67)

WHAT IS BIBLICAL FASTING?

1. Chisholm, Hugh, ed. (1911). "Gesenius, Heinrich Friedrich Wilhelm". Encyclopædia Britannica. 11 (11th ed.). Cambridge University Press. p. 909.

2. Edward Frederick Miller, The Influence of Gesenius on Hebrew Lexicography (Contributions to Oriental History and Philosophy, No. 11)(1927, NYC, Columbia Univ. Press), pages 14-15; Edward Robinson, Bibliotheca Sacra or Tracts and Essays (1843, NYC) ch. 6, 'Biographical Notices of Gesenius and Nordheimer', page 367.

3. "Gesenius's Hebrew and Chaldee Lexicon - Study Resources." Blue Letter Bible, www.blueletterbible.org/study/lexica/gesenius/index.cfm.

4. Gesenius's Hebrew and Chaldee Lexicon to the Old Testament Scriptures, by Wilhelm Gesenius, Bagster, 1859, p. 705.
5. The NET Bible: A New Approach to Translation, Thoroughly Documented with 60,932 Notes. Biblical Studies Press, 2005. (Note on 1 Corinthians 7:5)

IS FASTING NECESSARY FOR NEW TESTAMENT BELIEVERS?
1. Irenaeus. Against Heresies. Christian Classics, 2019. 2.32.4
2. New English Translation textual criticism note on Mark 9:29.
3. Kirsopp Lake, ed. and trans., The Apostolic Fathers with an English Translation, vol. 1, LCL (Cambridge: Harvard University Press, 1959)
4. ibid.

DID THE APOSTLE PAUL BELIEVE IN FASTING?
1. The Book of Acts, by F. F. Bruce, Eerdmans, 1988, p. 185.
2. Acts, by Darrell L. Bock, Baker Academic, 2010, p. 358.
3. Acts: An Introduction and Commentary, by I. Howard. Marshall, Inter-Varsity Press / IVP Academic, 2008, p. 170.

HOW LONG SHOULD I FAST AND PRAY?
1. New English Translation translator's note on 2 Corinthians 10:12.

HOW SHOULD I PRAY WHEN I FAST?
1. Thomason, Tim. "Blind Faith." YouTube, Blind Faith Foundation, 7 Sept. 2016, www.youtube.com/watch?v=DokWFR_FQS0.

THE FOUR APPETITES THAT MUST BE DEALT WITH
1. "2: The Science of Deduction." The Complete Sherlock Holmes, by Arthur Conan Doyle, Barnes & Noble Classics, 2004, p. 14.
2. Lake, John G. Spiritual Hunger. Christ for the Nations, 1979.
3. Pascal, Blaise. Pensees. Ale Mar, 2020.

THE DANGER OF THE DANIEL FAST

1. "Note on Daniel 10:3." Dake's Annotated Reference Bible: by Finis J. Dake, Dake Publishing, Inc., 2014.

WHAT WILL FASTING DO TO MY BODY?

1. "Chapter 4: Toxic Relief Through Fasting." Toxic Relief: Restore Health and Energy Through Fasting and Detoxification, by Don Colbert, Siloam, 2012, p. 47.
2. "The Joe Rogan Experience." Performance by Joe Rogan, and Dr. Rhonda Patrick, The Joe Rogan Experience #459 - Dr. Rhonda Patrick, 19 Feb. 2014, open.spotify.com/episode/1YK7KITyXL 8aa8ckMYeRgg?si=zK4qaS3lSTK_gMnDZyoI8Q.
3. McCarthy, Moira. "More Than One-Third of Americans Have Dangerous Metabolic Syndrome." Healthline, Healthline Media, 9 July 2020, www.healthline.com/health-news/more-than-one-third-of-americans-have-dangerous-metabolic-syndrome.
4. Galvin, Gaby. "America Has Gotten Much Fatter in the Past Two Decades." U.S. News & World Report, U.S. News & World Report, 27 Feb. 2020, www.usnews.com/news/healthiest-communities/articles/2020-02-27/us-obesity-rate-passes-40-percent.
5. "Obesity." World Health Organization, World Health Organization, 1 Apr. 2020, www.who.int/news-room/facts-in-pictures/detail/6-facts-on-obesity.
6. "Chapter 4: Toxic Relief Through Fasting." Toxic Relief: Restore Health and Energy Through Fasting and Detoxification, by Don Colbert, Siloam, 2012, p. 47.
7. "6 Tips To Be 'Water Wise' for Healthy Kidneys." National Kidney Foundation, 1 Sept. 2020, www.kidney.org/content/6-tips-be-water-wise-healthy-kidneys.
8. Lopez-Jiminez, Francisco. "Wondering about Fasting and Heart Health?" Mayo Clinic, Mayo Foundation for Medical Education and Research, 4 Dec. 2020, www.mayoclinic.org/diseases-conditions/heart-disease/expert-answers/fasting-diet/faq-

20058334.

9. Watson, Stephanie. "The Effects of Cholesterol on the Body." Healthline, Healthline Media, 3 Apr. 2020, www.healthline.com/health/cholesterol/effects-on-body.

10. "National Diabetes Statistics Report, 2020." Centers for Disease Control and Prevention, Centers for Disease Control and Prevention, 11 Feb. 2020, www.cdc.gov/diabetes/library/features/diabetes-stat-report.html.

11. Pratt, Elizabeth. "Experts Skeptical on Claims That Intermittent Fasting Can Reverse Type 2 Diabetes." Healthline, 15 Oct. 2018, www.healthline.com/health-news/intermittent-fasting-and-type-2-diabetes.

12. Landsverk, Gabby. "Will Smith Says He Fasted for 10 Days and No Longer Needed a Blood-Pressure Medication He'd Been Taking for a Decade." Insider, Insider, 27 Sept. 2019, www.insider.com/will-smith-fasted-for-10-days-off-blood-pressure-medication-2019-9.

13. "Frequently Asked Questions about Stem Cell Research." Mayo Clinic, Mayo Foundation for Medical Education and Research, 8 June 2019, www.mayoclinic.org/tests-procedures/bone-marrow-transplant/in-depth/stem-cells/art-20048117.

14. Trafton, Anne. "Fasting Boosts Stem Cells' Regenerative Capacity." MIT News | Massachusetts Institute of Technology, MIT News Office, 3 May 2018, news.mit.edu/2018/fasting-boosts-stem-cells-regenerative-capacity-0503.

15. Wu, Suzanne. "Fasting Triggers Stem Cell Regeneration of Damaged, Old Immune System." USC News, 5 June 2014, news.usc.edu/63669/fasting-triggers-stem-cell-regeneration-of-damaged-old-immune-system/.

16. Bray, George A. "Is Sugar Addictive?" Diabetes, American Diabetes Association, 1 July 2016, diabetes.diabetesjournals.org/content/65/7/1797.

17. Gellene, Denise. "For Rats, Sweets Are the Drug of Choice." Los Angeles Times, Los Angeles Times, 10 Nov. 2007, www.latimes.com/archives/la-xpm-2007-nov-10-sci-sweet10-story.html.

18. Greenberg, Melanie. "Why Our Brains Love Sugar - And Why Our Bodies Don't." Psychology Today, Sussex Publishers, 5 Feb. 2013, www.psychologytoday.com/us/blog/the-mindful-self-express/201302/why-our-brains-love-sugar-and-why-our-bodies-dont.

19. "Chapter 18: Fasting and the Body." God's Chosen Fast: A Spiritual and Practical Guide to Fasting, by Arthur Wallis, CLC, 1968

FREQUENTLY ASKED QUESTIONS ABOUT FASTING

1. Marcin, Ashley. "Intermittent Fasting While Pregnant — or Trying to Get Pregnant." Healthline, 22 Oct. 2019, www.healthline.com/health/pregnancy/intermittent-fasting-while-pregnant.

2. "Chapter 21: How to Break the Fast." About Fasting, by Otto Buchinger, Thorsons, 1968.

3. Gunnars, Kris. "11 Myths About Fasting and Meal Frequency." Healthline, Healthline Media, 22 July 2019, www.healthline.com/nutrition/11-myths-fasting-and-meal-frequency.

4. "Chapter 17: What About Asceticism?" God's Chosen Fast: A Spiritual and Practical Guide to Fasting, by Arthur Wallis, CLC, 1968.

SPIRITUAL BENEFITS OF FASTING

1. Noth, Martin. Numbers: a Commentary. Westminster Press, 2000.

2. Colbert, Don. Toxic Relief. Lake Mary, FL: Siloam, 2003. 155. Print.

3. Franklin, Jentezen. Fasting. Lake Mary, FL: Charisma House, 2008. 41. Print.

4. Bucholz, Roger, William Fields, and Ursula P. Roach. 20th Century Warriors: Native American Participation in the United States Military. Washington, D.C.: Dept., 1996. 1-8. 20th Century Warriors: Native American Participation in the United States Military. CEHP Incorporated, 1996. Web. 19 Dec. 2015. <http://hdl.handle.net/2027/mdp.39015055469772>.

5. Hampton, Bruce. Children of Grace: The Nez Perce War of 1877. New York: Henry Holt and Company, 1994, p. 216, 243
6. "Colonel Sanders Story." Colonel Sanders Story. Full Gospel Businessmen, n.d. Web. 21 Dec. 2015. <http://fgbt.org/Testimonies/colonel-sanders-story.html>.
7. Wallis, Arthur. God's Chosen Fast. Ft. Washington, PA: Christian Literature Crusade, 1968. 50. Print.

ABOUT THE AUTHOR

Evangelist Ted Shuttlesworth Jr. has been preaching the gospel for close to two decades. Ted has been privileged to minister across the United States, as well as in other nations, with many creative miracles reported.

Ted is an author, weekly podcast host, and the founder of Miracle Word University—an online training resource designed to raise a new generation of leaders and equip believers for their God-given purpose.

He is a graduate of Rhema Bible College and currently resides in Florida with his wife, Carolyn, and their three children, Madelyn, Brooklyn, and Teddy III.

PRAYER OF SALVATION

Heavenly Father,

Thank you for sending your Son, Jesus, to die for me. I believe that You raised him from the dead and that he is coming back soon.

I'm asking you to forgive me of my sin and make me brand new. Give me holy desires to pray and read your Word. Empower me by Your Holy Spirit to live for You for the rest of my life.

You are the Lord of my life. I thank you that the old life is gone and a new life has begun, in Jesus Name, Amen.

....

If you prayed this prayer, please contact us. We would like to send you a free gift, pray for you and help you take your next steps in Christ.

info@miracleword.com

GET STARTED WITH ANY
BIBLE COURSE FOR **ONLY $69!**

Finally, affordable online Bible training courses that will build your faith as well as your knowledge of God's Word and equip you for your calling.

We'll cover subjects like Divine Healing, Pneumatology - the Person and Baptism of the Holy Spirit, Answered Prayer - Understanding how prayer works & how to receive answers, Mountain-Moving Faith & Worship Keyboard

MIRACLEWORDU.COM

HOW TO ACCELERATE YOUR PURPOSE
THROUGH THE FORCE OF IMPARTATION

As God did with Moses and Joshua, Elijah and Elisha, Jesus and His
Disciples, and Paul and Timothy, He wants to use the power of impartation
to accelerate your purpose and destiny. Why start at the ground level
when you could receive a divine deposit that would place you head and
shoulders above the rest? In this new book, you will learn how God uses
the force of impartation to activate your supernatural promotion. You will
discover 7 scriptural keys to receive divine impartation in your own life
and ministry that will create supernatural momentum allowing you to
make maximum impact for God's Kingdom.

SHOP.MIRACLEWORD.COM
OR ON YOUR PREFERRED E-READER

When the children of Israel went into captivity, they hung their harps on the trees and began to weep. They locked their praise away. The very thing that had brought them victory so many times in the past had been kicked to the curb.

The enemy knows how powerful your praise is. That's why he uses a spirit of heaviness to steal it from you. Praise is the pathway into every blessing God has prepared for you. From healing to prosperity and everything in between, praise is God's prescription for victory. This new book will show you how to unlock the covenant blessings of Heaven through the supernatural power of praise.

SHOP.MIRACLEWORD.COM
OR ON YOUR PREFERRED E-READER

DIVINE PROTECTION BELONGS TO YOU BECAUSE OF YOUR COVENANT WITH GOD

It seems fear has intensified in America and around the world. Whether it's viral outbreaks of disease, the economic downturn of 2008, breaking news about groups like al-Qaeda, Boko Haram, and ISIS, school shootings, natural disasters that seem to be escalating around the world, or attacks like we saw in Paris and Brussels, the hearts of people seem to be filled with terror.

Should Christians be worried as the days grow darker before the coming of the lord? IS there hope and portection for God's people? I believe there is. This book will reveal how you can access the protective power of God Almighty, while the workbook will take you into a deeper study of your biblical covenent.

SHOP.MIRACLEWORD.COM
OR ON YOUR PREFERRED E-READER

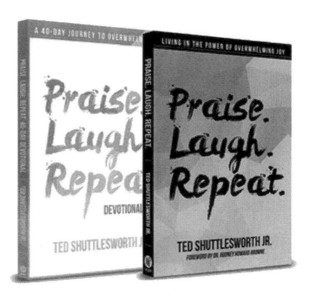

YOU MAY OWN THE FASTEST CAR IN THE WORLD BUT IF THE GAS TANK IS EMPTY IT'S NOT GOING ANYWHERE.

That's why the overwhelming joy of the Holy Spirit is so vital to your Christian life. The Bible tells us that the joy of the Lord is our strength. If the enemy is able to steal your joy, he has also stolen your strength and the momentum to do what you've been called to do. The Apostle Paul told the church that God's kingdom is made up of three elements: righteousness, peace, and joy in the Holy Spirit. Surprisingly, many Christians today are satisfied to only have one of the three kingdom components present in their lives! This book will show you that there are clear paths that lead to living a life of overwhelming joy. Don't allow the enemy to steal your peace and joy ever again. You can shed the skin of depression and enter into feather-light living for Jesus Christ beginning today!

SHOP.MIRACLEWORD.COM
OR ON YOUR PREFERRED E-READER

DOWNLOAD OUR FREE APP

you can hear preaching 24/7, watch our youtube
videos, listen to our weekly podcasts and much more

FOLLOW US ON SOCIAL

/MIRACLEWORDMINISTRIES

@TSHUTTLESWORTH

@TEDSHUTTLESWORTH

TED SHUTTLESWORTH JR.

Made in the USA
Monee, IL
07 June 2024

59577616R00148